A MEMOIR

Honey from the Ground

Soren Tae Smith

MELBOURNE UNIVERSITY PRESS

Melbourne University Publishing acknowledges the traditional owners of the unceded land on which we work, learn and live: the Wurundjeri Woiwurrung peoples of the Kulin Nation. We pay respect to their elders and recognise the importance of Indigenous knowledge.

MELBOURNE UNIVERSITY PRESS
An imprint of Melbourne University Publishing Limited
Level 1, 715 Swanston Street, Carlton, Victoria 3053, Australia
mup-contact@unimelb.edu.au
www.mup.com.au

First published 2025
Text © Soren Tae Smith, 2025
Design and typography © Melbourne University Publishing Limited, 2025

This book is copyright. Apart from any use permitted under the *Copyright Act 1968* and subsequent amendments, no part may be reproduced, stored in a retrieval system or transmitted by any means or process whatsoever without the prior written permission of the publishers.

Every attempt has been made to locate the copyright holders for material quoted in this book. Any person or organisation that may have been overlooked or misattributed may contact the publisher.

No AI training: Without in any way limiting the author's and publisher's exclusive rights under copyright, any use of this publication to train generative artificial intelligence (AI) technologies is expressly prohibited. The author reserves all rights to license uses of this work for generative AI training and development of machine learning language models.

Cover design and artwork by Nada Backovic
Typeset by Sonya Murphy, Adala Studio
Printed in China by 1010 Printing International Ltd

NATIONAL LIBRARY OF AUSTRALIA

A catalogue record for this book is available from the National Library of Australia

9780522881813 (paperback)
9780522881820 (ebook)

For my children,
River, Woody and Aaliyah

—his feeble hand a javelin threw,
Which, flutt'ring, seem'd to loiter as it flew:
Just, and but barely, to the mark it held …

—Virgil's *Aeneid*

Contents

1

Spring

I DIDN'T KNOW when I would be ready to write about it until the moment I thought about writing exactly that: *I don't know when I'll be ready to write about it.*

The itch to write that down arose suddenly, from nowhere.

Sensuous feeling of typing my thoughts out the way I used to in the before life. Secret joy of returning to a world that has been closed to me since my son went.

I didn't know when I'd be ready to write about it.

A literary feeling. I thought it would not return.

That joy feels bitter because I'm here writing and he's not. My so interesting, so humble, so beautiful son, who left at nineteen, a victim of a hidden war in my country, in my world.

It's a war I'm not ready to name because I don't know its name. I may not be ready to write about that or to write about anything other than that. But I can write. He had got to the point of making notes on his phone.

I never saw them. I was going to see them later. Now his phone is in my room, hidden in the cupboard, and in a compartment in my mind, where I can't see it. When I found it on his bedside table, its battery was already flat. I'm not going to charge it.

The coroner said, we only seek an exact time if there are suspicious circumstances. The best way to know, especially with a young person, is to look at the phone, when he last used it.

Black rectangle of doom, my son called it.

He hated the phone.

The joy of writing might be replaced for now by what they call survivor guilt (how glib and convenient to have a term for such a thing, a term with absolutely no value to me), but the pain and guilt of writing will be worthwhile if I could continue to fight that war on his behalf. That's what we do. We keep fighting on other people's behalf.

So I enter this thing called narrative, with pain, unsure if it's a worthy enterprise. Worthy enterprises look like bad jokes to me. They always did, but now my scales can weigh everything against a human life. Does anyone who has not lost a child know exactly how accurate my scales are? Perhaps not, but I don't care. I'm in good company.

And so is he. Among the dead are more people and many who are better than those now living, and many we continue with—Yūko Tsushima, Jesus (at least for three days), Muhammad, Socrates, Diotima, Diogenes, Yeats, Simone Weil, Rabia al-Basri, Attar, Jalāl al-Dīn Muhammad Balkhī, Mary, Jacob, Jonah, John the Baptist, Abraham, Joseph, Jonathan, Shakespeare, Seamus Heaney, Julio Cortázar, Borges, Kafka, David Foster Wallace, Moses—add any and all of your own friends or heroes or sparring partners here. These are just a few, named as they arose, and they do arise, often, as I sit here in my bed day after day.

I like them. They are vomited up from whales, they have speech impediments, they invent words, turn tables, interpret dreams, eat honey from the ground, they philosophise alone, they run into the street with a lamp and a water jug, screaming that they will douse the fires of hell and set heaven alight, because they are sick of hypocrites seeking God's reward or fearing His punishment when they should be seeking His Face alone, and they write innovative short fiction. They do all sorts of things. They fight the distractions of religiosity or art or commerce or what has long been called the world. They tell Alexander the Great to stop blocking the light, a favourite of my son's. They ask if a human is a featherless biped or something else. They hold their heads in their hands at desks, in the street and in caves. They play. They stutter. They are killed. They weep. And some of them weep for their own lost children.

For instance, Shakespeare lost Hamnet. And Abu al-Qasim Muhammad ibn Abdullah lost six, all of his sons. And God addressed his tears, *Verily, I have granted you a spring in paradise / So glorify your Lord, and sacrifice …*

In paradise, in the highest heaven, a spring …

And about those who taunted him, those obsessed with male lineage, those people who were sons of sons of, about them God continued, *Truly, it is your enemy who is cut off [not you].*

I say that now too. Morning and evening, I am saying it, saying it to faceless, innumerable, insensitive, imaginary hordes who are still among the living, those who are intact, who've always had it easy, who blame others for their suffering and deprivation, who are capable of ignoring and avoiding and neglecting people to death, those innumerable, insensitive, ableist hordes who—if they bothered—would exonerate themselves. And might, to my face, say *I cannot imagine what you are going through* (obvious) and who sometimes write on the internet that *a person who has lost a child has suffered the very worst thing imaginable* (questionable), and who clearly haven't thought it through when they say, *It is not natural.*

And I know that—if they bothered—they would pity me because I have not only lost my son but half of a cloth I was cut from, and he has lost his life and both of us have lost this world thereby.

This world.

But—*Truly, We have granted you a spring in Paradise … It is your enemy who is cut off.*

I say it several times a day. It comforts me to know that just down the road, next to 7-Eleven, they are repeating it too, dusk and dawn. Maybe because it's one of the shortest ones. But they are saying it.

I don't walk there. I stay in bed and run between the two hills, and a spring of tears wells up. There will be mercy but not in the way that I want. (We laughed about it just last summer: Kafka: 'There is hope—but not for us.') To hold my son again, to be held by him. Now one hundred per cent of my hopes are based in an intangible metaphor: yes, we hold each other even now.

Even now. I can't say the word 'still' because of the traumatic memory it triggers. I can write it. But I don't like to.

I wanted to tell you that not all helpless love is romantic or sexual. Majnun went mad for Layla, but—

But enough about famous love already.

Grief is love with nowhere to go. Grief is a ceiling as vast as the sky. People who have lost a child are in a glass dome and no one can touch them.

Sounds and smells rise from the street to my upstairs window. I have just spent a long month sitting in my bed looking at the buds on the tree. Hard, cold buds on a tree whose name I don't know, visible through rented glass. I've only been here for a month or two. Another *notice to vacate*, this time due to *the owner's son will be moving into the premises*. Feeling resentful of buds. So mechanical. It's not real spring. I'm undeluded. I know now Descartes' disgusting vision: mechanical nature.

My online friends tell me that they felt this way too in the first year.

I write a poem for my son and upload it to a bereavement forum, where I know it will be understood even by the majority, who are older and lost children who were my age, not a son at the springtime of his life like Rimbaud in his poetic zenith prior to the gun running and the gangrene. I write copious 'poetry' like this now, when I'm too traumatised or too tired to form full sentences. I call it 'The first spring'.

So much for the Poets
and their Spring
    (spit to the left)
and their Blossoms
    and their Bees
I believed in it too

    Now the buds
blind and mechanical
    don't burst
they perform
    like me
(three times to the left)

    Nature gives a convincing performance
when it's time to get to work,
gets up, puts petals on
    but it can't be a real spring
first since you've been gone

But I was wrong. When the buds slowly opened and showed white petals, and then fully opened, it was like magical snow all over the tree. Bunches and bunches of bunchy beautiful blossoms. Bees came. In the night I sat and looked in amazement at the blossoms, brilliant in the streetlight. A vision. Hours passed.

In a week or two the blossoms became loose, relaxed, carefree. Fluttering blossoms drifting into the street. I saw again with the child and poet eye. The truer I. Repented from my cold and ugly vision. I wasn't wrong before. Love. Spring. A spring in paradise. All that is not only possible but certain.

The voice of a young man rises up, a stranger in the street below. Laughing and talking to a friend as they walk. That other silence. Cigarette smoke suddenly settles on my bed. The smells of a life I don't know anymore.

The time of the blossoms is already passing. Pale green leaves start to overtake them. Some of the blossoms are losing their whiteness, their wedding dresses look drab now, like they absconded and hitchhiked here. The promise of the leaf. *Nature's first green*, etc. I'm so exhausted from all these promises. I want and that appals me.

I want my son back. Sure. Fair enough. But I also want to see what the tree looks like when it's all leaves. And my body starts to long for the warmth of spring while my young and beloved son is in cold ground. The living body is a traitor. And I want my rug to come, the one I ordered online in the middle of the night. I want to know what it feels like under my feet and see the cats roll around on it. And I want to tell my son all about these things.

This is what I think, as I sit here in my bed at noon, hungrily breathing the cigarette smoke that arose from inside the chest of a young healthy man I never saw, whose laughter and voice and smoke just rose and entered my upstairs window and settled around my bedcovers up here. This is what I think, while the tree competes with the writing, and delivery trucks go by without dropping off my rug. And the wattle branch I put on the grave last week must be wearing dry brown clothes instead of yellow pompoms.

And his twentieth birthday will soon not occur.

2

The Long Dream

MY LIFE always used to bear witness to yours. I'd invoke it. We were so similar and I was alive, decades later. So you would be too. I survived my teenage years, my twenties, my thirties. So you'd be alright. Just like I was. You weren't. Now the loss of your life bears witness to the fragility of mine. Maybe I won't be alright either. Maybe I never was.

It is the official first day of spring and more plants declare themselves by flowering. Things grow. Herbs protrude from fence gaps and state their business. I touch everything, smell everything. Even if they don't flower, by their shapes and gestures, they declare themselves. But the flowers … I walk in the night and find dark branches sprinkled sparsely with white. I reach and pull a branch to my face and smell honey. A possum crouches up there, pulling the blossoms to her face as well, and holding each one between two tiny hands and nibbling on it.

My heart flowers with grief. Pain opens out in an endless rose. I declare myself this spring too, for the first time, but no one sees. No one reaches me and pulls me closer to find out my secrets. The scent of earth and flowers comes up from inside me and dissipates into the night. I know that if you were walking beside me now I would die from happiness. God can't answer my unsaid prayer for your return, because it would harm me. My heart is a cold, damp camellia. I didn't fall on the ground when I found you gone but if you returned I would perish from too much happiness, I simply could not go on if that much joy were to flood my heart.

Borges wrote about it. Endless rose. *Rosa profunda*. When I was twelve, the smell of jasmine was indistinguishable from love. In the same hemisphere as Borges, growing up in the suburbs, dreaming of elsewhere. Stars. Pop stars. Ready to give my heart away to anyone. The long dream came. To find someone to walk beside.

It was you. All three of you. My children.

People disparaged me. Middle-class married women tittered to each other, yes, literally, in the streets in 2008 they tittered. It seemed that there weren't as many single mothers then and certainly not single mothers like me, who were also tertiary students and whose car's door handles had rusted off, and who did not have time for friends, let alone 'networks'. Those women didn't approve. Perhaps, in their world, only some women should have children and those children are first and foremost accessories to marriage. The male–female coupling was an obsession for many of them, valued above mother–child love, which is mostly pathologised. They didn't know and now—I admit it—I didn't fully know.

I had it all.

3

Plants

IT'S NOT magical thinking—more like painting by numbers. When your creativity is too low to do anything transformative, you can move plants around.

1. Take a piece of a plant from an important place and bring it back to your house and keep it alive in a drinking glass.
2. Look at it by accident.
3. It will remind you that the situation is real and that you are doing things to help yourself to cope with it, even if all you are doing is moving plants around.

Or, in reverse,

1. Take a piece of a plant from where you already are.
2. Take it to a place that you can't always go and visit. Leave it there. Go home.
3. Then you can think of how it's there in your stead. Remind yourself you are dealing with it.

This is a very old habit vis-à-vis graveyards.

Sometimes the plants might be extra beautiful. These are called flowers.

Flowers help.

I now know a portion of the world's population who refer disparagingly to another portion as 'the non-bereaved,' by which they mean the non-child-bereaved—the only thing bereavement will ever be associated with for them again, no matter how many people they have lost in the past or will lose in the future. They say, for instance, 'I was talking to a non-bereaved the other day …' or 'Non-bereaved will often tell you ….' In this context, it is a synonym for 'fool'. Not always. Sometimes they can surprise you. Sometimes it can be both.

Sometimes non-bereaved say things like, 'I lost my dog, so I know what you're going through.'

When I finally made it to university in my early thirties, my daughter was just seven months old. I started part time and put her in the childcare centre, thinking it might be good for both, if not all, of us. But I immediately got hooked on the idea of being what had been advertised to me as an adult. I regret that now, even now, while I'm halfway through a PhD, while I feel like a better person with my reading glasses on—I regret all the meals I didn't cook, how many times we ate toast for dinner, how many times we didn't have a family night playing a game together, which was every single night. But I was working towards it. Working towards and never arriving.

Later, when you went, I was still a student. It was the only way you ever knew me. Mum: someone who leaves the house and goes to a more impressive building with smarter people than us kids in it. Was it like that?

No. There were archways and ivy and botanic walks between us too. We had our own atrium and our own secret places in invisible libraries. We had our own secret architecture and wisdoms. You and I, we were like two old sages sometimes, sitting in our trashed shed among empty caffeine drink cans—with a tilt of the chin towards the world out past that busted steel door, or with a slight shaking of the head or a small glance we could dismiss the whole world's folly. Often, it included our own too. That's how sage we were. Together, we knew it all. I must have taught you that—to know it all.

I was smart because you told me I was smart. If you never told me I was smart, I wouldn't have been smart.

Sage. When you grew your first beard, you used to stroke it and say 'hmm …?', which didn't mean you were considering something. It was your funny and indirect way of showing your doubt or disapproval.

I soon went to uni full time, unable to resist, though I had two kids at primary school and my baby at the childcare centre. Having found something I could do, it was hard to stop doing it. There had been decades behind me of not being able. Of being unable and disabled. Houses and cars and school jackets and people vanishing, falling away, dishes piling up, falling, smashing. I remember our private joke, based on the Raymond Carver story you never got a chance to read but that I told you about. You'd remind me sometimes, when I struggled anew to articulate my frustration and overwhelm, or when you wanted to express your own:

'Everything is falling'. Yes, everything had been falling for a long time.

In case anyone is interested, which they never were before, here is an equation I have struggled to solve:

Your child's classrooms are not heated.

A school jacket costs AU$128 from a family business, whose business is to make your child look smart, and a uniform is democratic and fosters team spirit.

Some children of all ages cannot keep track of a school jacket or any other thing in their possession for a single day, for reasons too complex to put in the equation.

With or without a jacket, but especially without, your child's effort to exist at school every hour is the equivalent of other people's effort during an exam.

The average winter temperature is 13 degrees Celsius. It's windy too. Winter is very long.

No, it will not be in Lost Property.

Soon I was the first at the childcare centre to drop off my daughter and the last to collect, 8 a.m. to 6 p.m. And you were in after-school care every night, at the school that was a fifty-minute round trip. On one occasion, I arrived at childcare at 6.12 p.m., and they were all there shaking their heads, those employees who I called 'aunties'. One of them, the boss, was furious and shoved my daughter into my arms in open disgust. My daughter couldn't walk yet. Six o'clock was closing time.

I was always running late, often literally running. I often had to roll-start a car and didn't have time even to wonder why the battery was so often flat. I was so exhausted sometimes that I had to stop the car on the way home from picking you up from school to vomit. You three were my reason for living, despite my simultaneously hurtling down the one-way street (blind alley?) chasing my intellect.

In one of my first classes, I was told about Plato's cave. I always sat right up the front, not only on the days when I had the pram in there and had to rock it to and fro with my left hand to settle the crying. I took copious scribbled notes that I never looked at again. On this day, I didn't have the baby with me. The lecturer, a grey-headed man on tenure, suddenly singled me out when he saw what was on my desk. 'A mobile phone? You of all people!' He thought I was too spiritual for that because he had seen what I was reading.

In front of forty people, I just said the first thing that was in my head since that's all I've ever done. 'It's my only link to my baby in case childcare needs to ring me.' I don't remember what he said. I didn't know how to articulate our lives then. I was in a situation where I had no one to put for next of kin. I waited till my oldest child was over sixteen and then I put him. Borges said Kafka invented his own literary precursors. I gave birth to my own emergency contacts.

Later, when I asked for more critical feedback on my essay, he said, 'There are always areas for improvement. We can't all write like Henry James.'

I looked up Henry James. It wasn't a case of not having heard of him. Not everyone's life is that simple and straightforward. It was a case of not having any idea if I'd heard of him, read him or tripped over him. You know when it's been a few hours between breastfeeds or nappy changes, you don't just forget. But I didn't know if I'd read Henry James. In case it might improve my style, I read *The Turn of the Screw* (again?) and was nonplussed.

I also believed that he'd famously said, *A baby carriage in the hallway is the enemy of art.*

This statement was an inoculation. My immune system remains on high alert against anything related to this toxic idea. Art that is a baby's enemy or in competition with a baby is not worth having. Maybe I was tired—I remembered it wrong. It was Cyril Connolly who said that, in *Enemies of Promise*.

This philosophy is highly quotable but it has no past, no future, and an impoverished present. Not only that, since you can replace the word 'art' with the word 'housekeeping' in his sentence, I wonder about the sanitised view of art he must have had.

A baby carriage in the hallway is the enemy of housekeeping.

I'd rather scrape Weet-Bix™ out of the carpet in front of the gas heater for another twenty years than keep company with this idea. It reminds me of some non-bereaved.

Lacking a certain type of experience and unaware of that fact.

Arrogant, right?

I like to practise it in Received Pronunciation or 'BBC English'. You can even try rolling the 'r' or eliding it.

A baby carrrriage in the hallway is the enemy of arrt.

A baby cawwidge in the hallway is the enemy of aht.

I may be overreacting.

All the same. Must have been a joy to share cigars with Cyril Connolly and a joy to know Henry James, son of Henry James—men of letters.

A decade passed (here we are) and three weeks before I'm about to fall back into the default state of underemployment, I grade a student paper on Henry James. It's lyrical, personal, delightful. It's beautiful. It's brilliant. He can publish it tomorrow.

Will I ever have time to read more Henry James? My son won't. I don't know if my son even got a chance to hear of him. He never got the chance to hear me ask him if he had heard of him.

4

Nervous Is Mostly Over for Me

A FRIEND CALLS. He is reliable, funny and considerate. I walk outside after curfew and talk to him on the phone while the rain drips from eucalypts and their hundreds of leaves shine white from the dark wet ground. It is like the ground is strewn with silver or like when you find treasure in a dream. Become breathless from walking uphill.

Is this a romance or a grief memoir?

Neither.

He corrects my pronunciations, teaches me a thing, asks me a question. He knows I am a recluse.

Are you happy to talk? Or feel nervous?

Nervous is mostly over for me.

…

The worst has already happened.

…

There is nothing to be nervous about anymore.

…

I'm aware of the conversation happening between magnetic poles within me, one pulling in and the other pushing away. He was the one I called in the worst moment of my life, though I barely knew him and I still don't. He is one of the last to feel the weight of your body in this world, just as I was the first.

That's something, isn't it.

It hampers small talk somewhat.

An old story comes to mind.

A man was on the way to be executed. He passed by the executioner and said good morning.

Why do you wish me a good morning? asked the executioner. Don't you know who I am?

Yes, said the man. That is why I wished you good morning. You are as important to me as my mother.

But you don't even know me, said the executioner.

First you expect me to know who you are and now you say we are strangers. The truth is that my mother brought me into this world and you will take me out of it. So good morning.

In a way, this person is both. He is like the kind of mothers I've read about, because I called him when I needed someone to help me. And he is like my executioner because he helped me to bring about the end of my world. He helped bury my child.

It's nice to talk to someone, anyway.

The gum leaves shine so brightly in the night, when the night drips and the curfew has come and gone, and the street is silent except for the dripping, and a voice is saying, *How are the kids? It would be nice to walk all together.*

When I was a girl, I could never have imagined this person that I am and this world that I live in. It is as if I am now on another planet to the one I was born on and am a different person entirely. I am very far from home and closer every day.

5

Genetics Counselling

MY HALF-BROTHER rings me this morning while I am preparing for class. I am in the middle of reading a creative essay about anorexia, wondering if my students will find it useful. We haven't talked for many years. We didn't grow up together.

I had lost touch not just with him but with the ideas involved. And I had lost my phones, my phone numbers and his phone number. Everything was falling. And I simply did not know what kind of relationship we had or what a family was.

The reasons for this are connected to the other reasons, to what happened.

I loved talking to him. There was an awareness that I have more right and reason to be talking to him and him to me than with a random person to whom I'm not related.

Now I'm drawing a line under it.

My three children are always enough of the world's population. Any energy I have will be for them. For the three of them. Yes, even now.

But if there's any extra, I won't hoard it. And there is nothing like genetics to remind you of what a family is.

It was a few days ago that my surviving son and I sat in the online meeting room with a genomics clinician to discuss syndromes that cause sudden death. It's unconfirmed.

It is good to see my son. He is upstairs in a Zoom square and I am downstairs in a Zoom square, just like in Forster's 'The Machine Stops'. We are both exhausted all of the time.

I wake every day not knowing if any of us will wake.

Before sleeping, to have my bases covered, I say 'in Your name we live, die and live again' because I believe in the Resurrection. (*Do not say you believe, for belief has not entered your hearts; say you submit.*) I say it like the verbal equivalent of a fine-print disclaimer.

The genomics clinician asks if she can use the blood from my deceased son's heel prick twenty years ago. She can't ask him but I know what he would say.

I say that I don't like to make decisions on the spot. I will sleep on it.

Can you really still access that sample? I say, mimicking genomic specialists. *Access that sample.*

Yes, we should be able to, she says in a tone that means *definitely*.

How spooky. A heel prick is meant to test for a rare vitamin K deficiency in newborns that should be remedied immediately. So, naturally, it has been kept, identifiably, for twenty years. Can you imagine the vaults? Drawers?

If he had one, she adds.

I tell her that yes, he had the heel prick but he was born at home. ('Home' is an absurd exaggeration but let that be.) In that case, if he had it, she is confident that the blood from my infant's heel has been preserved and can be used for genetic testing.

The Third Reich. Rumpelstiltskin. I think I can guess your name. But Brugada is even more scary right now. Long QT. We don't know.

She asks for the address where my son was born and I tell her the name of the town but I can't remember an address.

She pauses, incredulous.

It was twenty years ago, I say.

You can't remember where your son was born? she says, not even bothering to disguise anything.

I've lived in maybe twenty houses since then.

And that's the least of it. If only she knew what had happened since then. If she could know how everything has been falling. I could bundle it all up in a bundle and drop it on her head and watch her face.

Being socially unstable and itinerant hasn't exactly helped my case (somehow the landlord's choices don't seem to factor in). It may even have been a cause or 'contributing factor'.

We don't know.

The house was on a long road, I say. I never received mail there. It didn't have roadside delivery. It was a long road in the bush, I tell her.

That isn't helping my case either. I stop before I tell her, *and he was born in a tent.*

It was always a matter of glee for my son, when he'd leave a door open and someone would snap, *Were you born in a tent?*

And he'd say, *Yes, I was born in a tent.*

The tent had a zip flap, though, so it could still be closed. A more beautiful tent you never saw. I made it myself out of a heavy green truck tarpaulin and marine plastics. I sewed it sitting on the floor with my two-year-old, with him pressing the pedal of a black-and-gold Singer when I said, 'Go!'

We've always tried not to be negligent of our duties.

Is that enough for you, genomics person who is here today to tell us the results of our coronially ordered checks but informs us that a genetic syndrome is a probable cause that has not yet been identified in the genes checked so far?

I recall the black under our eyes, the dreaded PE, the fatigue, the sick days, the lost jackets, the attendance awards for others and chastisements for us, the ableist slogan in every school newsletter that got wet and sticky and mouldy in the bottom of the schoolbag each week, *it's not okay to be away*. All that this person, who is an expert in what we might bear within us, may not know. Who is an expert in genetics but gets it wrong about who is a half-sibling. Half-siblings, of course, don't help my case either.

Upstairs, the death certificate does not state his place of birth but it gives the address of his death.

But I know where you were born. Within my absolute love.

Signs of death immediately appeared. I've been running from them ever since. I've been running from them so hard.

I've been laughed at for letting my kids swim in a lake on a rope so that if they disappeared under the surface I could quickly pull them out. I've been amazed that other people don't think their kids are about to vanish or that they themselves are about to vanish.

Tenuous life. Data the least of our worries.

Should I tell her that sometimes I can't remember my own current address or that I get lost on the way to the shop sometimes, or that I can't, sometimes, even recall which geographical state I'm in?—and that the main reason for that, these days, is actually not my genes but oppressive, judgemental people? And probably my genes.

6

Sons and Daughters of Abraham

DEEP EXHAUSTION.

Exhaustion in parts of me that I didn't know about until they were depleted.

To walk two blocks and buy a coffee and walk home is a big event. I can get back into bed with a sense of justification if not indignation. I've been outside and walked two whole blocks and bought a coffee in public. That's the whole day, unless I'm teaching. Teaching is almost the only time I'm upright other than on the coffee walk. I stand for prayer with difficulty. I spend all my money on Uber Eats, buying food for myself and the two of my kids who eat. I want to buy for him as well. I don't even notice what it costs and will just stop doing it if the money runs out.

Some grief casseroles.

The food lacks the nourishment I'm seeking, which would be found in food cooked for me by another. Especially if they cooked it knowing why I need it. My children need food with that secret ingredient, and they don't even know it. They need food with the secret ingredient *someone cares about my mum and supports our family.*

Your order is on the move! and *There is no need to meet your delivery partner at the door* doesn't do it for us.

I can still taste the bitterness I felt when my friend said, *I don't think you are ready for a real meal yet* and I ordered cold sushi for her and ate my fourth banana. My love in the ground, or not even in the ground yet, I can't recall.

Teary. Which is not like me, whoever me is or was.

The entrance of our house is filling up with brown bags that say *Tonight I'll be eating*. I guess that sums it up.

Reading about others who thank their families and communities for rallying and supporting and being there for them at such a difficult time and how they'll be forever grateful and how they have been held up during their darkest days and how moved they were by the loving tributes that poured in from … makes me feel physically sick.

A peer support person who answers the child bereavement support line, when I say how exhausted I am, says, with such kindness, I wish I had ten cents for every bereaved mother who gets a major illness within two years. Like I care.

I was talking in codes but we hadn't figured out our codes yet. We were friends but they say that you are not supposed to give birth to friends. I created my own family by giving birth to them. I was alone before that. Not everyone does this. Then I tried to establish a new language. It was very tiring. I couldn't find the floor and I know you couldn't find the floor and I only want to write this for people who can't find the floor. Because only we know what that means and how hard you can work to find it and not be able to find it and how the tragedy occurs because of it or during it.

The prescience scares me because, if I knew, why couldn't I do something?—but prescience is only to prepare you. That's all it does. It can't be expected to do more. Sometimes I feel like I don't have any language left anymore except the love in my heart.

We have a cat who was in the pound. She is small for her age and looks the same as she was when we rescued her at seven months old, the same age my third child was when I sent her to the childcare centre and went off to university.

Rescued is an understatement. The cat was in a glass-walled room of twenty or thirty cats and all of them were drugged daily to numb their instincts. Their instincts would tell them to fight or wail. She was on a high tower when I walked past on the way out of the room, and she lurched into my arms and clung to me like a koala. We were only allowed to rescue her by paying a hundred and forty-five dollars and letting them take her ovaries and womb out prior to collection.

This little cat hides every time we walk into a room, but if you pick her up she cuddles and holds on tight and dribbles. Your shirt gets rained on. She learnt to purr after a few years as well as drool. When she walks you can see her trying to find the floor. Every step she takes is an individual step. Each step is planned and carried out. She does not enter a flow state except when hunting, which she does for her family: us. She hunts for socks and presents them to us as small mammals or birds. Without a womb, she adopts us. She rescues us. She cannot find the floor but looking after others gives her comfort.

I looked it up on the internet.

Can you stop your cat from drooling?

The answer was no. You can't. But you can feel grateful that you have someone in your life who is so ecstatic to be with you that they forget to swallow their own saliva.

Sometimes she washes the socks, lovingly, and we wonder if we have been wrong about the hunting all along. Is she presenting us with an abandoned kitten, or her own miraculous newborn, and asking for our help to care for this small, precious life she has managed to save?

Do you want to talk or just chat? my friend says.

I want to ask why those two words don't mean the same thing anymore, as a linguistic diversion, but he won't know what I mean.

Chat ok, I write.

Because I'm talking to another friend at the same time. When I voice my feeling of neglect during child bereavement, she tells me in her maturest voice, with the authority of someone who has no experience, how everyone is just trying to do the best they can vis-à-vis grief and bereavement.

My view is a little different. I think a lot of people are malevolent satanic Nazis. In this I agree with my young son. Perhaps if he had grown, we could have found out if his views matured and then he could overtake me and critique mine but that will not happen.

Necessity. We are in its steel trap.

Is it the jaws of the cat gripping the mouse with the intention of killing, or is it the jaws of the mother cat who grips us just firmly enough so that she can carry us to safety? Or to just bring us a sock and arrange it on the carpet in a way she feels is most pleasing, intending only good for us?

Maybe I am even more hopeful than my friend. I don't care about the malevolent satanic Nazis because I believe in Mother Necessity and her merciful jaws. Their dinky steel trap is useless against her intricate, intimate and instinctive care. This is God's way. The most rahman and the most rahim. My son and I didn't always agree on that – he was deeply into the Old Testament and said to me once that if he went back on his vow to give up smoking, God would strike him dead. The dream of a stern father he had never known?—no, he was so much more than that, my son. A true reverence for the power that begat him, which had nothing to do with me or his father but was a providential gift.

My son has offered me the greatest joy and the greatest pain that I have ever known. At his grave, I tell him that. And the most profound love that I have ever known or will ever know.

Chat ok

Ok

How are you?

Alhamdulillah.

Last time we talked, this man told me that there are more than twenty-five ways of sensing the true feelings behind someone's alhamdulillah.

Can he sense bereavement in our chat? Can he tell by the speed I type it? He cannot, or if he does I cannot sense that he senses it. How many ways are there to tell if someone can perceive your alhamdulillah? For me, none.

When I cleared out my son's personal things from his flat, after pressure from housing services, there either were or were not signs of recent smoking there, prior to that Act of God.

Steel jaws clamped down on him and carried him carefully to a safe place before releasing him. I follow. I do not make vows. *Swear not.* I suppose not everyone spends a large part of his or her life trying to figure out to what extent it is okay to make a vow to God. Or, more secretly, perhaps many do. Childish vows too: *if you … then I …* And the sheer facts of fear and desperation.

My insomnia strategy as a ten-year-old: posit a witch at the foot of the bed. If I open my eyes three times, on the third time, she will kill me. What was wrong with me, with you? I called out to my mother again and again, in terror. I wet the bed like James Joyce. Was my heart racing? Did I have arrhythmias, epilepsy, possession? I am not a creature of the Enlightenment either. I couldn't care less about Freud.

Sons and daughters of Abraham, he used to say, with his New World sideburns, stroking his sparse young beard, preparing for a visionary voyage.

Indeed.

7

Seasons

IT'S PUFFER jacket season in Melbourne. In the outer west, puffer jackets come in many colours, red puffer jackets over saris, orange puffer jackets over kaftans, kids in blue puffer jackets, but the closer you get to the CBD the more black puffer jackets you see. All kinds of puffer jackets but all black. Melbourne has a horrible cold season of grey glary drabness and icy winds, which are not done by official spring and often persist into official summer. Puffer jackets are expensive and very warm. Because it's so cold today, I am watching YouTube in bed.

I learn about the now-famous climber who scaled a MacBook background and who lives in a van with his girlfriend and says that he climbs because *no great thing was ever achieved by being happy and cosy* but seems very happy and cosy in his van with his girlfriend and his very expensive jackets. I am not happy but I am cosy.

Some don't choose risk and few choose to be cold. It's a fact that only wealthy people can have puffer jackets because when you owe a few thousand on electricity and get constant threats of disconnection by phone, email and text for a decade, you can't really feel you can afford to save for a puffer jacket. Only if one fell from the sky could you have one. And after a while, there is a sense of repulsion for all those warm people being warm and walking around freely while you crouch at home next to the gas heater or in bed. There's a sense that even though you want to be warm, you don't want to be one of them. My landlord once told me that in China, at the border of Mongolia, where it was bitterly cold, she saw nomads heavily wrapped in newspaper and twine.

I remember a homeless man in the charity line, where I waited while my kids were at school to pick up my boxes of UHT milk, cornflakes, caster sugar and muesli bars, who told me once, *Give up, love. Stop trying to hold up this shit show. Renting's worse than homelessness. You're wasting your time. You won't get any help until you're homeless. Just give up, it's what I did, I'm much better off now.*

At home, I'd arrange everything on the bench and make it look like I bought it all. I never said I bought it, I just wanted them to feel like they had a provider somewhere. *Where did all this come from?* they would cry out. And I'd act like it was a rhetorical question. *I know!* And I felt I wasn't allowed to wrap newspaper around us when we were cold, but I did make ponchos out of blankets without a second thought. By 'make ponchos' is meant: cut a slit in a blanket with a knife and tear it to a hand's breadth, just off from the centre. That way it's longer at the back.

Eventually my son did find one on the road, a puffer jacket, and he wore it for a while, and then gave it to me because *it looks good on you*. I feel good in it. It is old, faded red and it's quite a thin one but big and warm. I love it. He sometimes found things on the road—beanies, a single glove, cigarettes. He walked a lot. Rambled and roamed, took God's Uber almost everywhere. I plan to keep the red jacket for the rest of my life. It smells like the time when my son gave it to me, when we used to sit out in the shed and speak of many things.

Our cat once peed on a high-end puffer jacket. What can I say? She wanted something soft, warm and comforting.

8

Clouds

MY MIND is cloudy. From immense shock and grief, black under my eyes, the roof of my mouth cold, in bed for days, leaden, as if trying to resemble your last days above ground. I am all of these things, cold, heavy, stiff, but I can never reach you.

A text.

What are you doing now?

I prefer the way this person texts suddenly like this—though it is more effort than it's worth to interact with other human beings, unless they are my children.

I have two hours free for a lunch

He offers to catch up if I want to catch up. I am not used to communicating so I make some garbled reply, which confuses him.

To be clear, I should visit family today or another day?

Today is good

Today I am with Necessity's sister, Mercy. They are not really sisters. They are the same One, and that one has shown me the gentle side. I get out of bed. It is a nice visit.

He reminds me of humanity, in all senses of the word—its existence, its capacity for fellowship, its inevitably earth-bound nature. He seems solid, intact, kind, human. I don't know what I am or what he sees.

As a bereaved mother, I walk around inside out, feeling shattered and immense. I spend a lot of time alone with my son on the other side. Now I'm anxious, my hands jumping around like fat little bunnies in my lap. Talking makes me sweat. But underneath it, I'm some version of happy to see someone today. I don't know if it's okay to grin and show my missing teeth at the sides. I suppose that it is okay. Yes. I'm happy. It is good to talk. Some energy returns to my body and I feel my face come to life as I talk. To life.

Survivor guilt, they call it. Sounds like a way of failing to understand it. The past is a mountain of sorrow streaking my windowpanes as I try to imagine that this moment I'm in now is real. To imagine the present moment is real would be to accept that I survived.

I forgot my dreams but since the morning (and it has lasted until now, midday) there has been a cloud around me, a protective cloud. Yes, I know the facts. But the facts don't seem real and they don't hurt me. Interpretation is suspended. All things are, but nothing is just one thing or one way. A cloud of possibilities and a vagueness to it that is the opposite of painful shock. A gentle cloud. Alhamdulillah. Who or what is that cloud?

I dreamt that I saw boots made of emerald

I explain *boots.*

Long shoes, you know

oh long shoes yes

Yes. And they were clear, beautiful, made of emerald

Emerald? What is it?

I use Google translate.

Zamard? Zamarad? I can't read it, no harakat

Let me see zumarud zumarud yes could be it means jannah allahu alim

My friend has asked me many times to correct his English, perhaps we could do a language swap, but how can I? I could no more correct a person's arms and legs or eye colour. We don't know each other well and it doesn't matter. I don't try to look behind people for a secret.

One day we tried to converse in a conventional way and he said, *What is your PhD about?*

I didn't want to say creative writing. It's jargon. And all writing is creative. I looked for the more general term for what I am interested in.

Literature! I exclaimed with relief.

Literature? What is it?

Um. Books. Literature. Books. You know. Literature?

I don't know, not sure.

Do you read books, I mean not fact books? You know. Literature? Alf layl wa layl

Oh alf layl wa layl no no no no no!

I don't know if it was just that he doesn't happen to like *One Thousand and One Nights* or if it meant he doesn't like literature in general.

It doesn't matter either way.

9

Reductionism (Shrinkies™)

ME AND my bitchy netball friend used to get them in the cereal box and the whole point of them was that whatever they were you could put them in the oven and they'd become small, powerful, concentrated, like the images on screens are now, like the two-inch people we scroll past, tiny but mighty and rich in attractive power in their intense compression.

But it wasn't like that.

In this life, it turned out that we didn't gain power by reduction, by being borne out of our dreams into smallness.

It turns out we are just small and powerless. These gargantuan dreams I had, these ideas that I moved around inside, like a child in a whirling amusement park ride, have brought me to a point that I'm now sobbing and vomiting out all that cannot be mine. You were all there inside my dream. The big names, I still remember them. The Aunts and the Uncles, the Cousins, the Baby. Grandmothers existed. Old People existed, People existed.

You will think I've just grown up. Maybe that's a valid way of looking at it but it doesn't sound like an explanation. No. It's a way of avoiding thinking about it.

I tried to stay asleep, like Jacques Brel said in 'La Cathédrale', the second-most idealistic song in the world, second to his version of 'La Quête', ne vous réveillez pas, but now not waking up means something completely different. Not waking up is what happened to my son.

We are small. Each and every one of us is a hedonistic megalomaniac narcissist. Inside our great dreams we see all the others moving around. Those big names. Mother and Dad. Myself. All those famous, famous names that set your heart racing. But a racing heart means something else to me now.

Now I hear of them, as each and every one of them falls, becomes a small man who used to cheat on his wife, becomes a wife, becomes a drunk, becomes mortal, a widow, a person renovating something, buying or selling or owning something. It's disgusting the way we keep doing that, shrinking like that, streaming into history like so much trash accumulating, blown back by the blast, like Walter Benjamin said about the painting he bought by Paul Klee, as they say mechanically in the university every semester. I spread my wings and watch, a little cartoon angel. Small as well. No way to resist it.

But what you put me in the middle of, my son, was not small and it was not history. It was the point of history, it was every cusp of battle and falling sword, it was every great tragedy there is. I was right there at the cutting edge of humanity. Love does not make trash of us, it doesn't.

Anon she finds him …

Virgil's *Aeneid.* From the speech that caused a fictional player to weep in front of Hamlet, and which I misremember as 'she finds him', because I'm thinking of Hecuba finding her husband slain, and I'm thinking of myself too, finding my son. There being nothing either of us could do.

I think of the love part. No. I think love is the only part.

It dawns on me that growing old is losing people. A baby hasn't lost many, which I guess is only right.

My heart breaks every time I remember a thing my oldest son said just once, in his excited voice (the only voice he had at the time), 'There are so many people in our family!' But a broken heart means something else to me now.

When Nan died at ninety-three, I spent a few days by the bedside. She was hallucinating that nurses were doing magic on her and that she was leaping out the second-storey window. She was in her right mind—dementia is first floor. It was the calcium or the morphine or both, they said. I prayed with care assistant Fatima in the wheelchair closet, using clean blankets for our prayer mat. It was a Catholic facility, chosen vaguely for its values.

It was many days before I discovered that she wasn't well. I witnessed her last words before she slipped into another zone and responded only to caregivers, by slight movements of the head or an indistinguishable sound. When I arrived, she was alone. I rushed to her and I said, 'God bless you, Nan!' and I said, 'I love you, Nan,' and she looked up at me with eyes purging thick amber and plum-tree gum and she said, 'I love

God.' A secret never admitted in that branch of my family of birth, a secret locked up in stuffed cupboards behind years of failed hopes in rooms ringing with conflict and alcoholism—

—but who wants to speak of that dark vision?

When we, my son and I, in a true dream, became golden and danced together in the rainy street.

And just think of all the beautiful insects and plants. The dream of a childhood and safety that can be recalled even if never lived. Wisteria, rose, jasmine, cicada, ant, loquat, resin, paperbark, bull ant, stinging nettle, soursop, buttercup—we found whatever we could and made what adults call relationships. All these brought news that we thought was important and wonderful. We had no other news channels. We were neither small nor massive then, we were just creatures in the world, before the ballooning, before the drastic reduction.

10

Fluttering

OH, POOR, poor Nabokov, squinting at index cards behind the wheel in the dark outside the seedy hotel, conceiving a man as different as possible from himself, naming him, and positioning him for tragedy. Index cards filling with fact and fantasy. The deranged eroticism of novel writing. Trying to create people.

But here, blowing in a breeze from an invisible source, a tuft of fluff at the edge of the bathroom mat flutters, announcing an invisible wind from under the door.

I think of you. You. You as that first flutter, as an instant of movement and frozenness, the horror I saw (did you know?), and the freedom and fluidity of memory, in which you exist. Not fiction but memory. This is what I recall every time I go to the bathroom and see that same tuft at the edge of the mat, fluttering in the gale that blows from the base of the door. I see it many times a day and forget it as many times, but that tuft is there continuously. It's so easy to forget until it isn't.

Poor Nabokov and his preoccupation with nymphs, butterflies, girls, developing novels, whatever. How fastidious was God in painting butterflies and not catching them? Oh my son, how many bug catchers did I buy you back then? It became a running joke. You would never have caught or hurt an insect. You'd lose the lids immediately, let the halves of the bug catcher lie separated among the toys on the floor. It was a dream merely—a dream that was sold to us. Inside the house, you'd imagine the bugs, then you'd go outside and never remember to bring the catcher.

You loved life and the life within life. You searched and starved for it until your final flourishes: *This is to certify that the below … shall not perish but have everlasting life.* You did the one thing necessary.

I'm thinking of the Martha and Mary, Luke 10:38, on the value of housekeeping, index cards, novel writing or whatever, relative to the numinous presence of Life.

You had so little time or resources, but you did the one thing necessary.

But how fastidious was that author, old and famous, not only creating the man but getting a girl for him, painting her out of words, and rolling names around on his tongue, labelling her, giving her traits and cross-referencing her traits and acts between cards. Girl on strings to push and pull deftly enough until she came free. In spare time, to pin the pretty insects. Him and his pins.

It wasn't like that for us, my son. No. Poverty becomes resourcefulness that some mistake for creativity. The mere tuft says more to me, honest in the way it flutters, there on the mat.

Like Nabokov, I conceived a man. But that man was real. A man for an instant—had you finished growing?—a man who lived and within me lives still, in flutters like that very first, five months pregnant. No, the first was a heart-related flutter—*Could it be? Could I be pregnant? Are you here?* And now the heart-related thought—*Is it possible? Have I lost you? Are you gone?*

The same eyes in the bathroom mirror twenty years later, swimming in bewilderment. Heartache beyond anything I could have imagined. Pain in the heart. A numb arm too. I went to the doctor because I thought I was having a heart attack. The ECG was normal. It was you I wanted to take to the doctor, you I wanted to be given a heart check.

I explained to the doctor earnestly, 'I should also inform you that I recently lost my son and I have severe bereavement which could be affecting my physical health at the moment.'

She just looked at me. Odd behaviour. Communication deficit. What to make of it?

At the roadside, in the night, your neighbours must have heard me say it to the coroner into the phone, *No autopsy. I request no autopsy.*

If your request is approved, you need to understand that you may never know what happened to your son.

The man I called was there, well dressed, respectful and calm, standing beside his companion outside your low brick fence.

You'll know, he said. *If you need to know, God will show you in a dream.* You would have liked this man.

After I asked God to show me what had happened to my son, God answered me with a few disturbing dreams, as though I was a radio between stations. Apples that were poisoned. Fainting and medicine. Then the real dream came.

I don't know if I was awake or asleep or in another place that God reserves for the most serious conversations, the most important dreams. It had the atmosphere of the inner sanctum, a sober realism—it was hushed, interior, a confession chamber, a place unlike any other place. No thought, no emotion, no self. No sight, no sound, no pain. In this place were two things: a beat and a rest. In this place a heart was beating and resting. I was nothing but attention, observing a loss of rhythm. Long rests in between beats. Too long. Beats too close together. Then too long. Spaces. That was all.

I didn't know, and I still don't know, if I was observing this happening to my heart or my son's heart. And I don't know what the difference is between our two hearts.

Microchimerism: a mother's body contains early cells from the developing foetus. Those cells remain there for life and can become various tissues. They can become brain cells, or they can travel to the damaged heart and repair it, even becoming beating cells.

Pop science is often comforting.

Nabokov's major literary failing was not being a mother of anyone. But I can't excuse him for the butterflies, whose lives are short enough as it is. My son never read him or trapped any of them, but he took a sincere interest in life and the life within life.

11

Houses

IT'S NOT magic.

You emptied out every house in the world without my help. We must have lived in twenty together, moved from twenty together. There was always the thought of the next one. In the photos, I can sometimes identify which house it was by an old plastic jar we kept pens in during that period, or by the colour of the wall beside the desk. Behind it, the teasing door frame of an entrance to a room that is no longer in my memory. Sometimes I don't remember which backyards go with which houses. Some houses I don't remember at all. Maybe it's your bedroom, where you cried yourself to sleep so many nights. Maybe it isn't. And now, as I drive past the random buildings, I notice how you have hollowed out the space behind every window, hollowed out every house, rich or poor, high or low, made them utterly empty of any prospect. I no longer care where I live because you won't be there.

Every time we moved it was such a big haul. So much work. You were so helpful. Up and down the goods lift at the storage place. We separated and reunited around identical hallways, laughing under security cameras. Oh, those would be the home movies I want. The security footage in that last self-storage place. On and off with the free trailer stuck to the tow bar, while we took turns bouncing hopefully on the axles and pulling at the weight of a car while I held the axle lock open. Don't hurt your back, don't hurt your back. Never thinking of the heart. Five loads to the tip. Watch your feet! The air lift at the back of the truck. Shared arrangements, asking you about logistics. Heads together. Working it out. We worked together silently as one, or chatting. Always enjoyed it as much as anything else on Earth.

I remember your father saying that he had helped his father in the tool-making factory that way, as a youth, always ready to hand him what he needed without being asked. He was still boasting of that twenty years later. Did it mean that much to you to be my right-hand man? You were like that with me in our single-mother house-moving factory where we were producing change, sometimes under compulsion, by necessity, and always because I imagined something better. We had no factory, no staff, no business, nothing to build towards for ourselves or each other. We worked for free. And every time it was such a haul and such a dream. Me on one side and you on the other. Levers, trailers, tow bars, trucks, hauling, tipping, balancing, throwing, lifting, sliding, shifting.

The landlords never got to know about it, never got to feel what I felt in my heart and the joy of being with your heart, or the stresses they placed on it. They gave us notices to vacate. They sent agents to withhold my bond and write *leaves on pathway* and *water in under-sink cupboard—return to wipe* and *dead fly on windowsill—remove.*

Overnight every single dwelling on Earth has been cleared. All the houses are emptied of interest and potential. I see their windows as I pass and know exactly what is behind them: nothing.

There is nowhere to move from or to.

There is no more work to do.

12

Death

I THOUGHT I would never be able to write about it.

That invisible force that pulled all the threads out of our rug and left some weft, some twine. The design is not gone but is it a memory now? What happens with it now? Was it the same design you saw?

To be blunt, if one loses a child, there will be metaphysics. This metaphysics will twang your ligaments and tangle you, hurt you.

There was our weaving. We didn't look at it much, we just lived with it, on it, in it, under it and through it. It had butter stains on it like a favourite book. It was dog-eared. We didn't always understand it. We grasped it. It was strong.

One night, an invisible hand grasped all of a certain type of thread in our weaving, all the threads that were you, and yanked hard, and swiftly our weaving came undone and out and gone went all of those threads from our weaving. I knew them suddenly as distinct. Many of them were what I had thought was me. I didn't grasp them before, not with my tendons and my heart. The rest of the weaving went instantly old and slack and fell from the weft. Twine is harsh and sharp, I reach out to touch what is gone and pull back. Where you were.

I love this harsh sharp twine weft, I love it, it is the only thing I love more than whoever made it, and more than you. I love it with my life. It is all I have left.

Seamus Heaney tells me on YouTube that T. S. Eliot described it like this: 'in another pattern'. It is the last reading he gave for 92NY, on 26 September 2011, a day before your tenth birthday. Seamus becomes confused. Does he misquote? Perhaps thinking of memory, grief and love, he keeps calling his book's epigraph an epitaph. 'What could be used as an epilogue uh—no—an … epitaph … no—ah. Yeah. [laughs at the irony, audience joins in] An epi—epi*graph* for the new book was something beautiful, lines from T. S. Eliot, which go—from "Little Gidding": "See now they vanish, the people and places of the self, which, as it could, loved them".'

Not quite. I looked it up.

But the confusion is apposite.

—See, now they vanish,
The faces and places, with the self which, as it could, loved them,
To become renewed, transfigured, in another pattern.

He must be reciting it from memory. Does he misquote? Or is it within him in another pattern?

Just before you went, I'd sent you a link to Heaney's 'Digging'. I became obsessed with it that day. We talked on the phone. I think it was our last conversation. I was sitting on my bed. I said you can really feel the feeling of digging. If you know what the feeling of digging is like, I'm not sure if you do. You laughed, yes I do, I do know what digging feels like. Now I think I could hear in it the gravelly sound of what I'd be doing a few weeks later, until a young man tried to prise me from the shovel and my task. Sister, he said, will you share? Share, he meant, the blessing of it, of giving due rights to the dead. I was the only woman there. It was a polite way of trying to help me stop. Gravel. Shovel. Grave.

I don't want another pattern unless it's connected to the old one. I'm staying like this, entangled with you and us and Heaney and those people and places and that self.

13

Death

THERE WAS too much death.

I felt us spiralling down the plughole of Necessity. I think he felt it too. We were both panicking about it. Worrying was inevitable but it didn't help us. I was spinning my wheels. For a long time, my worry showed itself like irritation, frustration and anger. What it was, to me, was being wrung and wrung and wrung and the fear or feeling of losing what I loved the most.

I was wrong not to show nothing but kindness.

As a single mum, I thought I had to show strictness sometimes or it would all go to mush.

But now I think, to hell with that.

And I think, I was right to be afraid.

Once the wringing out finally snapped through my gut fibres, once I saw what I'm sure is in the category of the saddest, scariest, worst thing there is to see, I knew I had been right to be afraid.

It's selfish to be afraid. To think only of your gut fibres and how much wringing they can take and what their snapping will mean and how long that will take to heal. (After giving birth, the second time but the only time with you, I felt my abdomen and there was that long gap between the muscles where they had parted, where I had surrendered my strength to give you room, and it was only a few days ago that I felt for that gap and it was gone. That sign of the strength of my absence of strength, my ability to accommodate you, was part of me for more than a decade. It gave me a certain access. I wanted to press my fingers again towards where I once felt your head bulging under my ribs but the muscles have finally woven themselves back together.) It's selfish to think of one's own fibres. You were right about that. Even though it's the worst thing, it's also bad to know I wasn't kinder to you during those years. I repair it now with my daughter and I have to layer on the sweetness and it feels too much but I realise it's not even enough. My standards are shot, there is no machine translation service or conversion table such as we can access for currencies and time zones.

INPUT: Parent with My Background Gratitude Response: *Ok good, glad you got there safe*

OUTPUT: Parent with Loving Background Gratitude Response. *You are so thoughtful and responsible to let me know you got there safe. I trust you to take care of yourself 100% but thanks so much for checking in with me! I love you so much, have a good time beautiful one <3*

Response successfully converted.

I would have consulted it regularly. I wanted to do better. I never wanted to repeat the past curse, genetic or otherwise.

That's part of the curse. Wanting to do better. An understatement for scrambling desperation.

There were so many almost-deaths as we swirled around the plughole of Necessity, from that first somewhat worrying word, 'transverse,' that the midwife said (echoed later in you saying you didn't want to be born and that not ever having had to be born would have been perfect—the saying of a young person, and naive, but there was wisdom in that, as in so many of the things you said and did), to the sound of your brother saying from the bathroom 'The baby's under the water' and I still remember pulling you out and putting you over my shoulder and knowing the narrowness of the escape.

All those disturbing dreams, mine and yours. Mine, of having a child a few centimetres in size and losing him somewhere or putting him in my pocket and then remembering hours later, in shock, that he must have suffocated in there; of realising I had a child and not knowing that I had forgotten for days—dreams of neglect, forgetfulness and sudden shocks. I dreamt these even before I became a mother. Then the recurring dream of my children drowning and me pulling them up out of the water. Someone with a fancy turban interpreted it: 'When you pull them up it is you raising them. It is your anxiety about being overwhelmed and not being able to raise your kids. The heavy water is the world.' It sounded reasonable. I went with that. But the size of the turban does not equal the size of wisdom, otherwise he could have just given me the turban to wear. But I know what it was really about—it was a dream about losing you. I have a literal mind: the first thing I did when I came to your house that night was to check in the bathroom.

I always, always feared accidents for us. It culminated in the fire.

I can't talk about the fire. There was fire coming out of that plughole and it scared me. It forced my hand. I don't like it. A blackness had tried to claim you while you were asleep, had crept so close to your head and swooped in under your sleeping body. You weren't going to wake up. You always had trouble waking up but who can you tell this to? Who will listen to this symptom? My child doesn't wake up properly. When I pitched your gutted mattress into the pit at the tip, I saw how close it had come and indulged myself in imagining we had escaped yet again. I wasn't convinced, though. I thought we had escaped the way a child gets candy and therefore believes that everything is alright.

And when I moved to that house, where these precedents happened, many more than I can tell, I remember clearly the voice inside me.

It was the same voice that spoke to me that final night, before I had decided whether to drive to your house, and I was thinking, *I should think about it in the morning, or probably his phone is just out of battery, or maybe I should just go to bed and stop fussing and worrying so much*, and the voice said calmly, 'Just drive there now.' And when I got ready for the drive to your house and I was thinking, *Shouldn't I be hurrying if I am so worried?* it said, calmly and clearly, 'It doesn't matter if you hurry now. You can take your time getting ready. Either it's fine or you're too late.'

And then it said, as I reached my hand out towards coat hangers, 'Wear something you don't like much. Whatever clothes you choose, you will never want to touch them again.' It was a voice like my own, but completely pure, a perfectly clear transmission in the long space between heartbeats.

Yes, that was the same voice that had spoken two years back, when I moved to the last house we lived in together, where the precedents happened. The house had an address that was very unpleasant, that aroused any and all superstition renters might have about numbers and names and locations, and since they often live in hardship and misery, they have many. But it wasn't superstition. The voice said, 'After you move here, either he will get better, or he will die and it will be over.'

It is not a voice you question. It is the voice of Truth and Necessity. But I know I am not the only one who has heard it when it comes to life and death situations. When it comes to love.

I heard Bilal Assad on social media describe how uneasy he felt in his heart as he stood beside the snow mobile in which sat his brother and young son. As he watched them drive away on the track, the voice said, 'They're going to smash into the wall and they will die.'

It is not a thought. It interrupts your thoughts with its voice.

After the fire, there were a few more near-death moments for you. I don't even know about most of them, but one I remember clearly, as if I have the back of your shirt between my fingers even now.

Housing services had said to me they could find you accommodation in a couple of weeks, while I contested an unlawful Notice to Vacate during a global pandemic, having lost my casual job and having imagined that you would fare better without me. I invoked the story of the youngest son who goes out into the world inheriting nothing but a piece of rope but manages to catch his fortune. But months passed and you were living twenty-three floors up in some interim hotel tower on King Street, waiting to hear from them about something more permanent. Meanwhile, I moved house without you, to something distant and cheap, and took your existence for granted, imagining on the basis of zero evidence that you were at liberty to do the same.

You rang me and said they had finally allocated you housing. I looked it up on my phone, zeroed in on the entrance.

Your first place!

'It looks great!'

It was such a relief to both of us but you said it was just as well that it had happened now because you hadn't been doing so good. I didn't know that until you said it. Part of me recognised it as one of your classic understatements but this awareness was not fully conscious in me.

It was moving day.

'How will you get your stuff there?' I asked. The owner of a HiAce.

'Oh I'll get the bus or whatever.'

'I'll come and help.'

'Oh that's okay, no stress.'

'I'll come and help, it's no worries.'

'Thank you so much.'

You had tried to talk me out of it. I wasn't even sure if you would want me to, or if Independence, that fruitless American dream, had taken over our lives to some unknown extent that precluded this particular involvement by me at the cusp of your seeing your first place. How stupid can I get?

How stupid can I get?

And I was equivocating. City driving is not easy for me. *Not easy* is one of my classic understatements. I struggle to find my way out of my own house. I get lost on the way to the shop. And my thoughts were interrupted. Something told me, 'Get in the van and drive. Go there.'

And so I went there and waited outside until you came down. I remember seeing you. I remember then that we went up the twenty-three floors and you showed me the balcony. You had been living there for months without me, but when you leant on the rail, my heart went wild and I reached out and gripped the back of your shirt between my fingers.

That's not enough to save you. It's only enough to reassure myself you were safe. And only at that moment.

Dear son. Let my prayers not be like that.

Again, I visit that swimming lake at a picnic ground, holding two ropes in my hand, with you and your brother swimming there. I don't regret holding the end of the ropes. Strangers sneered or laughed and failed to discover how sexist they were (controlling female, etc., fussing mother, etc.). But the surface was opaque. I just felt it, I felt the fragility of all of our lives, especially yours.

One of our family stories: the first time your brother saw the sea, he cried and wanted to get back in the car. The first time you saw it you ran straight in and were planning to keep going. Into the grey waves. I pulled you out, held you back.

No, it's not true that I felt the fragility of your life more, or not all the time. We took turns.

I couldn't afford all of our lives to be fragile at the same time.

The touch of that shirt, that centimetre hold I had on your precious life that day, on the balcony of the twenty-third floor where housing services chose to place a vulnerable teenager during lockdown, while I managed yet another Notice to Vacate from a landlord, is so sweet and so fine to me. I wish I could hold on to it for the rest of my life.

And maybe I'm too harsh on myself—the main point of getting haptic feedback about your position on Earth was not only to reassure myself but so that I would be ready to make extra effort if and when you needed me—ready to hold you in both my arms and pull you back from the ledge, from the fire, from the rental house, from the streets, from the bad people, from bullies, from water, from what both of us knew about and from the horror that all of it was swirling around for your whole life, and faster and faster for that whole decade.

14

Women's Legs

THERE IS an early surrealist text that inspired Kafka. It's a case of stating something so explicitly or repetitively that one feels the absurdity. It's called 'Women's Legs' and I can't find it anywhere anymore. As for my own legs, they have been able to push the heaviest furniture around the room but have always felt explicitly, repetitively and absurdly weak when climbing slopes and stairs.

I remember driving one of the old cars down the gravel road after dropping the kids at school. It wasn't a day when I was so nauseated from fatigue that I had to pull over, or a day when I couldn't climb the steps to the childcare centre. It wasn't the day of the floods but it was that same gravel road. It wasn't Black Saturday but it was close to that year.

Memory and trauma are clouds, fog, mist, dust, heat haze. They are not machines, clocks, timers or calendars. But it might have been the locust year, the year they sizzled in the grille of my car and polka-dotted the road with dark shiny patches like a chewing gum epidemic, and the rhetoric was propaganda-like as if warning us about a dangerous underclass. As usual it was war rhetoric too. It was a battle against insurgents. We had been given a pamphlet by the school. It referred to the locusts as gang members, *the juveniles form marauding hordes*, etc. They were insects.

We laughed about it in the car. You were gifted. Even at that age, you understood so much.

Later you said it was because of me, as if it happened because I fed you royal jelly, so to speak: 'I am intelligent because you told me I am intelligent. If you hadn't told me that, I wouldn't have been.' I don't believe that, but I get your point. I treated you like an adult—but only through my own incapacity and inflexibility (internalised ableism: I mean, through my socially imposed disability)—and, whatever the reason, you were old by nineteen. On that night, I entered the flat of a retiree, Bibles on side tables, your gold-rimmed glasses by the bed, your making do with a cracked lamp by the bedside. You'd walked yourself to church only days before in a suit. Decency. Uprightness. Righteousness. You had that and you had plans for more of it.

Few of your friends met you in your final iteration. Living underground like a cicada for seventeen years, you had emerged. I got there too late, found the shell. Ringing in my ears. Now I remember the brief moments of your juvenile uprising and insurgency, the early signs: the unmistakable hordes that formed at that time. One of them, a gigantically tall girl, hugged me in the hallway of your impromptu birthday party that had become too big for my Kafkan introversion. I scuttled back to my room. And I remember your voice on the phone as I sat on the concrete outside the shed door, 'I might be living away from home for a little while.' Might. Little. Forever understating. Understating, I didn't know, can be fatal.

I went to your room and looked around. I wasn't ready, I hadn't even started. I hadn't even started to take care of you, raise you, live with you. I cried so hard, smelt your T-shirts, I cried so hard and for so long into your T-shirts that my heart was a wrung-out rag. I knew it was a kind of grief. I didn't know it was practice.

I didn't know, either, that you didn't know how I cried like that, loved you like that. I thought it was obvious. I never said, 'No, come home, please, I love you and miss you.' So obvious. I was so understated that I said, 'Oh, okay,' which meant 'No, come home, please, I love you and miss you and am worried sick.' You learnt understatement from me. Or we both learnt it from our world in which our voices were unwanted and unwelcomed.

It was a world in which imitating others' voices was our only option but those voices had nothing to say that could match up to our life or our needs.

The locusts. That was when you were a primary school kid in the country, with the green and gold uniform, and I was a single mum driving you there and back, over gravel roads, out to the corner where the old iron school bell still hung, and was even rung for recess and lunch (I chose the school for the bell and the trees; later you approved of these motivations, I smugly recall). It was the phase between being harassed, vilified and frightened for my life for leaving, and when your father died of the slow suicide that is lung cancer in some heavy smokers. (Looking back, I remember night sweats and the wrong kind of cough decades before the email that said 'three months'.) On driving back down the gravel road, I noticed, for a few days in a row, that there was increasing talk on the cracking car radio about single mums.

I never listened to news. I guess I just wanted to hear a song. But the words 'single mum' seemed directly relevant, unlike almost every other thing I heard. There were callers to the station. People were giving their opinions.

'I don't see why they can't just work like everyone else. Me and my wife both worked.'

I had never realised before that the hatred of my kind was strong in my own society. I didn't know. I was shocked to hear some of the things people said about me. And how much they didn't know about me.

I was over thirty.

I didn't really know I was a single mum.

I was fighting for our lives.

What's the name for the other people in the family? For the people who weren't there?

For decades I never used the term and then I started to use the pompous term 'sole parent', which I learnt from official documentation. Then I realised that by using that term I was erasing myself. I'm not a parent, I'm a mother. I want to draw as much distinction as possible between myself and the fathers in this country who receive amazement and admiration when they raise or 'mind' their children, even for an afternoon or while their mother has a nap or gets some jobs done. And 'single' is also a strange word for what I am: forced to flee from events that happened before my birth, with my sons' father prematurely dead from the legacy of underacknowledged trauma and, yes, that official result of *lung cancer*. He was involved in certain shades and shapes of violence that were waiting there for him, and then for me, before we were even born, and which made me a single mother. Eighteen years older than me, and me with such understated parents that the question 'Why didn't you even raise an eyebrow?' was answered with 'Well, you never took no for an answer.' What that is code for, I can't say.

Within weeks of the split, the government department representative on the phone said, tentatively, 'To be honest with you, it was the strangest phone call I've ever had in my life and I've been working in child support services for a long time.'

There was no help with the problem at hand, but there was a payment to keep us housed and fed. And that still means choosing food by highest caloric value to lowest cost ratio. Or by weight, if you're on foot, which my son was.

The two-dollar stale-tasting yesterday's Glad™-wrapped coffee scroll was my main meal for the day at uni while breastfeeding, etc.

And the radio broadcast as I drove home from dropping them off—I still remember the female politician said, 'If they couldn't support their own children, they shouldn't have dropped their knickers in the first place.'

There was debate over this. Over which women had the right to get pregnant. And which women should have been more careful or, perhaps, celibate. Which women, in fact, it was implied, would be better off sterilised. An American Nazi ideology—yes, see California's *Asexualization Act* of 1909, 1913, and 1917 to 1979, and see also *Buck v. Bell*, 1927, not yet overturned—based on economics. Based on nice neighbourhoods.

My mother said she would have liked more children than just me, but *expensive*. And did her fake-shudder routine.

I would have liked at least five.

When I look back, I know for a fact that it wasn't primarily the lack of funds that hurt us. It was being an unacknowledged underclass while being blamed for being members of that underclass, while trying to raise children to respect themselves in those conditions and doing the job of a whole village by myself. That's what hurt us. More than hurt us: damaged us fatally. We did not consent to it and we did not create it. It is not a family or a society that acquiesces to it: it is a filthy tank of piranhas. Real illness and death resulted. Anyone who participated in it should be tried.

Now let me tell you what I really think.

We ate a lot of pancakes. Flour and water and, when possible, egg. Staple. We had real maple syrup because even if you are quite poor, sometimes you have fifteen dollars. It lasts a long time and will make any pancake taste good. If you have butter, so much the better. If you have fruit. If you have a clean plate. If not, eat out of pan. Also, you should make ghee by heating butter and clarifying it. It's easy and better for all cooking because it doesn't burn or smoke.

Another staple: delicious yellow dhal the neighbours taught me to make. Your favourite food thereafter. Here is the recipe they taught me one day.

Chop and fry an onion in oil if you have an onion
Pour in some orange lentils
Add water
Add salt (a lot)
Boil it until it's soft
Add curry powder and turmeric
Mix in some milk or yogurt or coconut cream if you have any
Eat it with some rice or bread

I might as well share this because I may never cook it again. It smells of family, of hope, of life, of love, of nourishment, of dreams, of motherhood, of the best and worst years of life, of you, of all three of you, of a time when I thought we'd get out alive and together. It is all there in it. I can't.

Sometimes I see the last half-cup of this orange dhal in the base of the plastic container at the back of the cupboard. I can't touch it.

And the other one from that time. This is all-day breakfast.

Heat a lot of ghee (butter ok but it burns a bit) in a very small pan
Add ground brown rice and fresh cardamom

Stir it and brown it
Add water, brown sugar, and random fruit like chopped bananas, apples and if you have it you can add dried fruit like raisins or sultanas
Simmer it without stirring till it congeals like a porridge and then browns at the bottom of the pan. It should separate from the pan. Don't be impatient. Wait longer.
Turn it upside down on a big plate and sprinkle cinnamon and nutmeg on it
Pour maple syrup or honey, some almonds you roasted on a dry pan and smashed up
Pour a dash of milk over it if you have it
Spread a cloth on the floor
Get four spoons, sit cross-legged and call your kids to come and eat it and they will come from wherever they are and they will love it because nothing has happened yet and the internet didn't get invented yet and you'll sit around in a circle with your spoons biting away at the full moon of it, biting away towards emptiness as if time were a friend

I heard another reference just the other day.

I was in the Colombian café waiting for my coffee. There was a newspaper. I don't normally look, but I flipped through it and saw that a politician, a woman, was being told she should resign over what she said in Parliament to another woman about her legs.

She had allegedly screamed to the other politician, 'At least I keep my legs shut!'

According to the other woman, this was an unwelcome reference to her fertility and the fact that she had borne an autistic son.

The article focused a lot on the recipient of the invective and on her autistic son, even showing a photo of the mother and son together to enforce how much she loves him and is glad that he has been born—when, in reality, something else had happened.

Only a three-line paragraph makes it possible to know, at least it does if you remember being a ten-year-old girl and looking across the room towards other girls as they sit cross-legged on the mat or up at their open-fronted desks. The woman who had said it, who was already in the middle of the kind of undignified slanging match that is normal in Australian Parliament, may have momentarily thought she was a ten-year-old girl again. She had forgotten all about fertility and sex, let alone disability. 'It was nothing to do with that. I just saw something disturbing across the room and I shouldn't have said that.'

This is the country I live in.

She had seen the other woman's knickers.

I only wish that the woman I heard a decade ago on the gravel road, the politician who cut the single parent pension and sent us further below the poverty line and deeper into invisibility and precarity, whose assessment of my right to be a mother humiliated me publicly and induced agoraphobia and shame, on top of the violation and threat I was already managing, and on top of the ever-high vigilance and cortisol, and made it even harder to shop, harder to walk, harder to sleep, harder to live, harder to cook, harder to express my love, would have been so contrite. But she wasn't.

We made a joke of it, didn't we? You and me? If I was overwhelmed, stressed or we just ran out of petrol or milk or money or were confronted by one of the many vicissitudes of single-mum life, or I was frustrated by something you'd done and saying, 'But why can't you just—', facing problems we couldn't solve, my son and I, we'd look at each other and nod with great sagacity. We'd have the epiphany the society was waiting for us to have. Shouldn't have dropped those knickers in the first place. Yes. That's it. That's what it is.

I'm so glad that, in so many ways, in between blaming each other, we didn't blame each other.

Next week I will sign the first job contract of my life and, for ten whole months, I'll experience not being unemployed or a casual worker. I won't be a farmhand. I won't be looking after other people's children, picking grapes for other people's wine or hazelnuts for other people's restaurant desserts, or dragging a bag of bulbs trailing pesticide down my leg up the steep hill to push into the dirt with my aching thumb for your supermarket flower bunches while my breasts fill with milk, or cleaning other people's houses while my children are at school and will come home to their own dirty house so I can provide passive income for a landlord with family money. I won't be making the beds for other people's holidays and setting their fireplaces with symmetrically placed pinecones for their cosy evenings with their families or friends. I won't be standing all day sorting out strawberry runners frozen together in clumps of dirt at a factory shelf or taking over a real employee's high school classes, breaking up fights and stopping them from blowing pen ink into the carpet and raising the chairs above their heads or trying to yell over the top of them to tell them what I've been instructed to say while your children say back to me, *Where the fuck is our real teacher?* without expecting an answer. I'll be a real worker now.

I never worked harder than when I was a single mum, and I never worked harder than when I was unemployed either, doing all the jobs of all the other people who weren't there for me or for my children, and who remain silent and nameless about this fact to this day, even if they are talking to each other about it, even if they are talking in Parliament or on the radio.

15

Conceptions

TWO DAYS ago, I had occasion to drive past the place my first child was conceived.

'That's the exact spot,' I told my daughter. 'Take a photo!'

I didn't mean it was the exact spot where the event leading to conception happened. I meant it was where it dawned on me.

'That's where my caravan was parked, on his block of land,' I told her. 'It was where I went down that hill from the house and said to myself, I'm pregnant. I was twenty-four.'

My daughter, genuinely interested and not at all judgemental of this prehistory, or perhaps no more than one judges the activities of extinct animals, happily took many photos.

It wasn't just that I was driving. My daughter has a better phone and camera.

I remembered lying there, on that spot—well, suspended a metre from the ground in the now invisible caravan—with my hands on my flat belly and feeling the distant vortex of Necessity, as you, my first child, descended through the spheres from the source of Life, towards little old me.

I noticed, on that exact spot (and they couldn't have known), in the large clearing, the current occupants had put a cluster of flower planters and watering cans.

We drove to places where my second son hadn't been conceived yet, where he was living his dream of not being born. Fair enough. And I liked that sense that there was all that future ahead, the joy of meeting him, knowing him, and maybe don't think of some of the other things that were going to happen.

Then I drove to the town nearest to the heel prick in the tent.

Of course, I couldn't find the actual back road or gravel driveway and I didn't try. But I was in the region.

'Take a photo of the clouds!' I said. I was reading the half-forgotten calligraphy of those hilltops against the sky. I knew we were near. 'Send it to me!'

I never had ultrasounds with my first two children but with my daughter I was so sick in early pregnancy that I thought that maybe I had contracted a disease. I had constant terrible thrush and pain, and urinary pain, and a nausea that seemed close to psychosis. I didn't even know who I was. So I arranged it and went to check if it really was just a little baby.

I told her, 'I looked over at the screen, and there you were, waving! You spun around and put your arm out like this.'

Later in the day she handed me her phone and went to pose on a little bridge across a river, my precious daughter, and I took the photo and she called out over the sound of the rushing river. 'My boom pave!'

'What?' I yelled.

'My moon wave! Was that my room wave?'

'What?' I yelled.

She thinks I'm going deaf but it's just difficulty with audio processing and grasping things without context.

'Mum!' she said as she collapsed against me, laughing and grabbing her phone, and spun back and threw her hand out.

Yes. It was, it was her womb wave!

'Send it to me!'

16

There Are No Waves Down Here

IT HAS been almost nine months, as I wrote this morning on a bereaved parents' forum, since I carried you in my heart. It is not just a convention among bereaved parents. It is real. We know it and feel it, or some of us do. And sometimes, when it's too much, it's an elephant sitting on our chest or a backpack full of bricks, this new pregnancy. But on the days when we can bear it, it is exactly that. Carrying you in my heart. For almost the same amount of time now as I carried you in my womb.

We are not at all put off by clichés. We find them comforting. Walking in each other's footprints, knowing we are not blazing a trail, we are not the first to lose a child and we will not be the last. You are not alone. A day at a time. Remember to breathe.

At first, a lot of people said things about waves to me. Waves of grief. I think it comes from a bestselling book I haven't read. I didn't know what they were talking about. I still don't think I do.

I have been underwater my whole life and this just sent me deeper. There are no waves down here.

There are cycles everywhere, though. There are times when everywhere I go my eyes well up with tears and I am on the verge of crying. I seek exits from wherever I am and sometimes I have to remember to breathe, and I calculate times. That I can be out of Woolworths in less than five minutes if I leave now. That the car is just down one escalator or the house is just two blocks away. I don't mind if I cry a bit in the street, but not in the shops. But lately I am starting to notice a cycle of feeling hard and a bit mean for some days in a row. Snappy. Then I realise it's been a while since my eyes welled up with tears. Then I realise that soon they will. Then they do. Because I tell them it's time they did. One time I went all the way from the land of hard and mean to find myself weeping into your blanket and holding it as if it were your body. It was a better place to be than the mood that came before. Was that a wave of grief? I can't imagine it like that at all.

As with everything in my life, I imagine one day I will be in the middle of where everyone else has always been, and I will say, 'Yes. Now I know what you mean. Waves of grief. Waves of grief. I get it.'

I know I am slow.

17

Certificate II in Retail

I HAVEN'T ASKED if you turned up on that Monday to the government-mandated online Certificate II in Retail. I'm not even sure if they would have the record of that anymore. Maybe if I call to ask if you attended, they would tell me what one of your schools said when I rang to say goodbye, years ago, after a time of relentless bullying by some students and some staff. 'Well, if he's leaving, you have to fill out the exit form.'

I said, 'I know, I've done that, I'm just ringing to let you know we are going.'

She snapped, 'But you can't just go, you need to submit the forms.'

I didn't understand why it seemed so often that people couldn't hear us, and I said, 'I have submitted the form and everything, I'm just ringing to say that it's done and he won't be coming in anymore—' and then she said, by way of goodbye, 'Oh alright, I'll delete him from the system.'

I believe it was the last time we spoke, how you said that you had learnt something from the Certificate II in Retail after all. That no matter how you feel, if you make a smile with your face, like when answering the phone, you sound happier to the other person.

The last time we saw each other, you almost declined to meet because of that government-mandated online Certificate II in Retail. When we did meet, we cut it short because you had to get back to it. If you hadn't attended, you wouldn't have been able to pay the rent.

A certain Monday was the last day of that course for my son, who was reading Dostoevsky's *The Death of Ivan Ilyich*, among other things, when he passed away alone two days later.

18

At the Bus Stop

AT THE bus stop, in Footscray, when we saw the bus come around the corner, I stood up. You hoisted the heavy crate of spring water, on which you'd spent your last dollars because it made you feel better in a way you had mentioned but hadn't explained to me and I hadn't properly asked.

The bus pulled up.

I said, 'I love you.'

I couldn't change anything.

'I love you too,' you said.

'I'll see you soon,' I said, pointedly, knowing it had been too long.

You smiled affably and nodded agreeably and stepped on to the bus.

Sometimes there are no goodbyes. I know this.

There may be a mercy in being stopped mid-conversation because the conversation keeps going. No closure. Ever.

19

19

OVER IT is nineteen. 19—

These are the letters whereof only God knows the meaning—

A common note of commentary upon the Muqatta'at, the disjointed letters.

By the pen, etc.

There are codes. Collections. Pokémon. Gaming.

I would literally give you a million dollars for that coin—

I only thought it would occupy you, you know, but I forgot the internet—

you don't know even know—

I think you are getting too much into the biblical numerology—

you nearly did me in with that coin—

like the Aleph—

I'm sorry—

I shouldn't have looked at your notebook, I thought they were lyrics—

~~Eighteen~~ Nineteen years and I haven't had much to say. Falls on deaf ears anyway—

don't worry, the coin is mostly just Hebrew stuff and good things but it's very strange that Nan had it in her bedside drawer—

we are not responsible for the sins of our ancestors, how can you believe that?

how can you not believe it?

I feel bad—

So tomorrow is my nineteenth birthday and I was thinking of coming up and hanging out with you for the night—

[Did you think I didn't know?]

Mental shackles—

Are you okay? Delete that. Hi. Delete that. I miss you. Delete that. What are you up to?—

listen, when I said that, I didn't mean it literally and I wasn't talking about your father, I'm so sorry I said that, I just meant it in a general way like haven't we all been raped by the devil in this society, in this world, I'm so sorry, that was such a horrible thing to say and no child wants to hear their mother say a thing like that, I'm such a fool!

I'm glad you said this actually. I thought you meant my father—

oh no—

writing, art, sure, whatever. You can write all the weird crazy random crap that goes through your head but—

[I can't remember the rest of that sentence but I will permanently remember this writing advice from you as the best warning I ever received about my literary art. I cannot promise to always make sense but I'll try.]

birthdays can be very hard. Some grieving parents have their child advance in age relative to their siblings or as if time passed for them normally. Others feel that their child is always the same age as they were when they passed away. There is no right or wrong.

Jesus was 33—

What age will my brother be in heaven?

In heaven we will all be 33—

I think he will be 19.

20

Quiet Hour

RECENTLY, AFTER the mild torture of shops all my life, one of my sons told me about it. They turn off the music, dim the lights, clear the floor trolleys, stop the announcements and allow us, at last, to shop in peace. Or so I've heard.

I imagine fellowship. I imagine autistic people, hyperactive kids, babies and single mums, bereaved people, PTSD sufferers, old people, fewer working people (the shops don't run it after hours). We'll all make our way through—perhaps to the sound of screams from the still overstimulated toddlers, for whom even a muted shop is a bad idea. If I could give any advice to a new mother it would be: never take your kids to a shop. At all. Any shop. No place of business. Just don't do it. Ever. For your sake and their sake. But what choice is there?

Up to now, I haven't managed to get there for Quiet Hour because I only remember it when I am in the shop thinking if only it wasn't so bright and loud. But lately they've increased it from one hour a week on a day I don't necessarily remember, and which is within business hours, to every day from 10.30 a.m. to 11.30 a.m.

It's 10.35 a.m. now and we've been out of toilet paper for three or four days. I found a quarter of a roll in the car last night flattened under the seat. I found some kitchen paper. Quiet Hour inspires me.

I'm going to get dressed and find out this secret thing in my society that seems to cater to my needs. In a society designed by people with mostly different needs than mine. It seems so strange, this public declaration that their environment is bad for a lot of people.

I told my son I'm going and that it's great they are doing it every day at the moment. He laughed because he saw it as a business decision: if they don't do it, there are people who hate the Christmas music and crowds so much that they will simply not shop in what we call 'the lead-up to Christmas'.

I'll be back in a minute with or without toilet paper.

I got there and the lights were bright. Then I heard the music, if you can call it music. Someone was screaming about being good for Santa, someone was crooning about war being over, and I realised something was wrong. I thought it must be that they had forgotten to do Quiet Hour. I couldn't concentrate on the fruit so I went to the registers to check the signs. Quiet Hour is from Monday to Friday. Today is Saturday.

I did a lot of shopping. It was horrible. I nearly cried. I looked at the Carman bars and remembered offering him one in the car and saying to him, 'Have a Carman bar,' and he took one and said, 'Thank you. I respect that,' meaning that he liked how I had organised a supply of convenient high-quality nourishment in the sleeve pocket between the front seats. 'Car man bar,' he said, and chuckled.

I also had some flashbacks to the last time my son and I were together in this world. It was the last thing we did together. We went to Woolworths and it seemed like a stingy little shop, but I convinced him to buy a sweet potato and instructed him gently and happily about vegetables, telling him you don't even need to do anything with them, you just cook them and add some salt and they are nice. He was agreeable, funny, sweet, beside me, and I let him pay for his stuff while I paid for mine and then we left. So hopelessly inadequate I am and it was. Why was it this way? Why did Necessity …?

Knowing all the time …?

As we walked through …

And I had to stop myself.

Santa, tell me.

All I want for Christmas is you.

The Victorian government requires that you wear a face mask when moving around outside your home. Please, Victoria, look after each other and stay safe. This is a message from the Australian Government.

The cats in my house are more mature than I am.

I was a child. On that day, I was a child. I didn't turn to him, in that Woolworths, and say, you are my best friend. I can't do without you. You make even this dismal and repulsive environment seem like the best place on Earth. I don't know it now but I will never be as happy again as I am right now, convincing you to buy a sweet potato that two weeks later I will be finding in your fruit bowl on top of your fridge and throwing in the bin and you, my love, will be where?

Emergency services will have left your bedside table where they moved it out of the way, your phone still and black on its edge, a rectangle of doom, and your pillow on the floor where they tossed it.

It was the day I said *see you soon* to him and goodbye to myself but I didn't hear that goodbye at all.

Tell yourself that your loved one has gone home ahead of you and you will soon be home too, or that you were on a journey together, and for whatever reason they have gone on ahead and you'll be meeting up with them at the destination. Otherwise, you will feel too much anguish.

I will try for Quiet Hour again soon. Maybe next week. I got two different large packages of toilet paper, one has the advantage of double length so I don't have to change the roll often, and the other seemed cheap and a bulk buy, so maybe I won't have to go there again for a while.

21

At the Tip Face

HE SAID, I wish, I wish, I wish I could just live at the tip. I feel so good here. I feel free.

There was a raggedy cat living there, sitting on top of old whitegoods, watching the cars passing in and out, watching us. We wanted to feed it. We reasoned that it must be finding food or it wouldn't be there. I could see he would have swapped places.

I can't write it now.

22
Flowers

THE FIRST was the small chain of daisies made of glazed metal, white and yellow, my favourite necklace as a child—

buttercups from soursops or so we said—

roses my mother said her grandfather loved but she never saw the appeal.

I love roses with real love—

growing gigantic and diseased out of our last front window and visiting us through the cat-gap, blooming huge and red, reminding me of God—

and thorns the same size and shape as the cats'—

never mind the bougainvillea that we called boganvillea, scentless flowers neither pink nor purple, unappealing, its stalks shooting high into the sky, twelve feet above the shed, I kid you not, its tendrils creeping through the whole clothes-line and into the shed window's louvres, the cut branches, when I tried to please the landlord, getting lost in the long grass and capable of sending us to hospital, thorns long and hard as shards of stone. Planted by some homeowning fool with more dollars than sense.

We joked about it together, that its only virtue—

jasmine—

you allergic, me in love with it—

the cat allergic too, every night waking me up by boxing it to the ground—

I don't take it to your grave, even though I'd like it there—

but I'm glad you no longer suffer from the constant allergies in this horrible city, the worst city for allergies and asthma in the world the hospital staff told me, when your brother nearly died, and you said it felt like knives stabbing into your eyes half the time—

silky oaks golden at their time of year, showing themselves to people who can't identify trees when they are not flowering, announcing and reminding of the times we reached up to tap the flowers on our palms without picking them and licked off the watery sugar-nectar, you and me, we loved it more than the other two—

as much as I do—

a great delight, the silky oak—

bottlebrushes from my primary school days, always a bit disappointing after you've touched them and wondered about them—

my friend said old people like flowers, they are really drawn to them, it's something about getting old—

I love them, I said, I am drawn to them, my whole life—

but she ignored it, yes the old people love them, she said—

I saw in that moment that she didn't and I became wary—

and another friend too, it happened—

I wish I could move to the rich suburbs, if only for the flowers, I said, the foxgloves and those huge purple spikes, and hydrangeas, oh my God, I said—

later, house-hunting for another rental, I said, I like it there too but there aren't many flowers—

flowers don't matter, he said—

flowers don't matter?—

flowers don't matter?—

They don't?—

Angiosperms don't matter?—

he wants nothing but pines and cycads?—

so much for him—

neroli, orange blossom—

the white flowers also on lemon trees—

and frangipani and—

suburban geraniums, red purple orange-red lilac—

alyssum from the base of fences—

scrappy in my suburbs—

fresh and wholesome in the middle-class yard fronts—

I wonder if he noticed all the flowers when he walked for hours—

walking and walking—

I never walked like that—

some men do it I think—
    and they drive like that too—
    your father loved flowers as much as I—
    the snowballs I remember—
    he brought them back to me from the far east—
    from his visit to his well-off roots—

he drove and drove like that—
    where are you now? I said into the phone the night he left,
he in a phone booth—
    I am going to drive until I run out of petrol—
    That's ridiculous—

Where are you?—
    I ran out of petrol—
    but where are you?—
    I don't know—

Did he walk as well? Only in the bush—

I just go to bed—

roses—
    old-fashioned roses that have scent—

    wax flowers that feel like wax—
    a marvel—
    that have strange dry leaves—

rough I think—
and smell strongly of nothing but themselves—

nasturtiums I found alongside a creek where I walked neglected for hours—
I did walk for hours—
I walked and walked under bridges and through muck—
flood warning—
do not dump rubbish—
running down drains two steps to the left, two to the right, two to the left—
jump the dirty stream—
neglected-child dance—

highways above—
that's what it looks like under them—
sticks exposed with reedy stinking false cobweb hanging—
flies—
flood warning—

no flowers there—

then mulberries—
nasturtiums again—
I'd get so far from home I'd wet my pants—
temporarily glad of that warmth—

Picked them and followed instructions in a book—
You can use nasturtium flowers or petals or rose petals—

back when I was still capable of following instructions a little—

at nine years old—

a tiny adult form of an adult I would never be—

separate, it said, *the egg yolk from the white*

by pouring the egg back and forth into its shell halves

discard the yolk (as if!)

whip with caster sugar until frothy

using a basting brush

brush the egg white mixture onto the nasturtium leaves and flowers

you can use rose petals and other edible flower petals if you like

use the lowest oven setting with the door slightly ajar

for an amount of time I don't remember

They will be crisp, sweet, and shiny—

and you will not remember how they taste—

but only the solitude of a beautiful world—

in regard to the events of the future—

oblivious—

in a peace that may return again in aching old age—

in forgetfulness—

Then—

when you were born, a camellia from my father and a carnation from my mother—

both, independently picked & chosen, pink—

on the bed beside us—

you new—

One day I'd like to say it to her, what she probably wants to say to me—

but I don't because it would insult (internalised ableism, hers, mine):

You're a lot like him, you know, my father—

a forgetfulness, like the oblivion—
and the traumatised in-between that hears—
what speaks clearly in the language—
of the flowers—

And red rose petals strewn—
where we had lain you down—

23

Alternate World Fictions

IN THIS one, there was the conversation we had on the phone where you said to me, I swear, if I hadn't got up and walked to 7-Eleven for spring water and drunk all of it, I was going to die. A hundred per cent, I just knew it.

What? What do you mean?

I'm not even joking. I was going to die, for sure.

What do you mean?

. . .

Were you sick?

You, laughing, I was going to die for real. I knew if I didn't get up right now and walk to 7-Eleven for spring water and drink it all, I would die for sure.

But why? Did you have a fever?

Ah not sure, not sure.

Was it a flu? What was it?

. . .

Like a flu?

I don't know.

The conversation of a minute maybe, on the phone. I was sitting cross-legged on my bed, in a different house, the house where you visited me and from which I visited you. The house of back and forth. The house of the minor crisis, the major crisis and the catastrophe. The house where I was when …

But are you okay now? I ask.

A hundred per cent.

But are you absolutely sure?

Oh one hundred per cent, one hundred per cent.

And you just laughed about it, and I laughed a little too, because we were both pretty much aware of how much you tended to worry me, and how worrying your life could often be for you as well, but I said, seriously, seriously, if anything like that happens you have to tell me! You have to call me!

For sure, for sure.

No, I mean it. Promise me if anything like that ever happens again you will call me straight away. Or call an ambulance.

No worries at all.

And we must have spoken of other things then, a beloved mother chatting with a beloved son. So many conversations eclipsed, only these fragments leap out like fish from that heavy water.

Then I said, what are you doing after this call?

And you said, ah not much, not much. Bit of reading.

Alone in the world, apart from one or two. Your pastor and the retiree at Bible study who calls you her son and promises to get you work as soon as lockdown lifts. Having changed your life, lost your Facebook password, lost everyone …

They'll think I ghosted them.

It worried him.

If they are reading, please know, that wasn't the case, he just lost his password. Even though he was planning to get out of Facebook permanently at some point, he didn't ghost you.

But I didn't hang up then and let you go back to reading.

I'm coming over with some food and drinks, I said. See you in twenty minutes.

And then I rang back and said, actually, I have to stop to put oil in my car, I'll be an extra ten. And I may be out of petrol.

No worries at all, no worries at all, Ma. It will be good to see you.

No time like the present with car oil.

True, true.

The warning light has been on for ages.

And then I drove down that highway in the daylight and when I got there you said at the doorway 'Welcome to my presence' and smiled your radiant and mild smile down upon me, and we hugged lightly.

I looked at you carefully to see if you were sick. It was hard to tell. You seemed fine. We spent some time. I noticed that I felt whole and complete in your presence and that I always felt like that and this time I told you. I've always felt so whole and complete in your presence. It's the closest thing to happiness that I've ever known. You said you felt the same. I wondered out loud if all mums and sons felt like that and you said, who knows, who knows. We chuckled. We ate the food I brought and agreed that it was delicious. I said, I've got something to show you, it's a surprise. I got you to follow me outside to our van, which I'd parked in your carport even though it was always stressful to park in there. I opened the back and the sunlight streamed in and illuminated a hundred litres of spring water.

Is some of it for me? you cried.

All of it is for you, silly! I said.

You were overwhelmed. Thank you so much, Ma.

And you recovered yourself and reached out to heft one of the pallets.

No, no, I said. This is my treat. I'll bring it in, it's no problem. How about you go and pack up our stuff while I unload and come with me, so we can drive back together and get your brother and sister. Then we'll all come back here and watch something together at your place and have a sleepover if that's okay with you.

On the way back I took a detour and bought you the Kindle you asked for months ago. You hardly ever ask for anything so I knew it was important and acted on it straight away, and we returned to your house with family members, food and drink, and the Kindle. We drank abundant spring water. We found something to watch that was interesting and funny and not inane or evil.

And I made a doctor's appointment for you and the next day you said don't worry about it, that you were absolutely fine, but I insisted that we go, and so we went to it and the GP looked at our cheap clothes and lack of fashion sense and strange communication styles (like he can talk) and thought it was probably drug related or something but I insisted that it wasn't the case. Then, based on my son's age and gender, he said it was probably caffeine drinks but I insisted that he hadn't had any caffeine drinks recently. And he said it was probably nothing but to come back in a few days if I was still worried. But I insisted. He said it was mental health and that anxiety was very common but I insisted. I told him, in fact, I would not be leaving until he did an examination and ordered tests.

Finally, with his mask and plastic face protector in place, he put on gloves and condescended to take your blood pressure. He did it grudgingly but he didn't tell us what it was (my fantasies can only reach so high). He had a face I couldn't interpret. But he wrote out a thing for some blood tests. I knew he was trying to get rid of us. I said, 'I'm not laughing or leaving or taking his or your word for it that he is okay. Last night he was afraid to be alone and I pulled the couch in next to his bed and slept there, because he was unwell in a way I can't explain, and I am so deeply, deeply concerned and have so little to go on that our lives depend on you paying attention right now. I wasn't sure if he would wake up in the morning, that's why I'm here. Pay attention, fool. The inconvenience and annoyance of my existence and my son's existence in this room is all we have right now. I'm not a doctor. In short, I cannot tell you how all sits ill about my heart, are you reading me?'

I insisted we do an ECG that very day and so we had one done. And when the nurse listened to your heart it was obvious that you had been understating everything and being misunderstood so drastically for such a long time and suddenly he saw you as a person and the whole world started to move in harmony and the ice of a decade thawed and we were swept along and they referred us to the hospital for a cardiac ultrasound and urgent further testing. We are suddenly safe. Everyone is so kind. AWF.

AWF.

The supermarket was out of red roses today, probably because it's Christmas in a week. And you still haven't given your Easter speech. You were due to give it in a few days but you spent the nights of Easter in the tomb.

The speech, your portion, is when Pilate comes outside and says, 'This is the man.' Now I have an idea of getting a big sprig of this native shrub that is in flower with violet-coloured pompoms from across the road outside a church you've never seen. I'm getting up now to get dressed to take some of that to your resting place.

I don't know what else to do in this world.

24

A History Like Ours

A HISTORY LIKE ours, who could ever know it? It's a secret, what our lives have been. There is more in it than in novels by Umberto Eco or plays by Shakespeare, though Shakespeare does come close. I suspect that in those last months, my son refrained from telling me that W. S., whose initials he shares, was on the bad list. The growing list of sell-out Satanists and quasi-Satanists that he recognised in our society and its annals. I'm not far behind him there but he was right to hold back on it, more tactful than I've ever been, knowing how dear those plays are to me.

The only people from my crew that he excused in this particular regard were David Foster Wallace, Franz Kafka and he was on the way to figuring out Dostoevsky. Mario Bros. were goners, which was deeply sad for him. He never spared himself pain, he wanted to be rigorously honest about the society that raised him and what it was up to and had been up to for the last thousand years or so. He recognised that it was abnormal. He recognised that it was mostly evil. He also knew it would never be able to recognise him for what he was.

'I can't see a future for myself here,' he said on the phone, in one of our last conversations.

He didn't mean he could see one elsewhere. He meant, with the best intentions, and after trying many avenues, he just couldn't see one at all.

Don't worry, there are so many other places, said I, who still imagines plane trips as mythical or magical events.

He had been on a plane only once in his life and did not remember it. They were things that went over us in the sky.

I went on a plane just a few times. Only once as a paying customer; the other two times, flukes, and without my children. Flown to a court case where I unwillingly facilitated a man putting himself in jail, and another time flown to a conference where I had no business being.

They are things that fly over us in the sky.

There are so many other places, said I. So many places better than here. So many possible bright futures for you. So many opportunities. Honestly. Really. There are.

Was I smiling when I said it, so as to sound happy?

I had just got my first suitable job when I said it. Casual but suitable. I could more or less cope with it and do it and get paid for it and keep doing that for cycles of weeks at a time. I didn't know with what I would pay rent over the summer break. The landlord could give us two months' notice at any time. I couldn't see a future either. And it was true. The person I was had no future.

I should have told the truth so he wasn't alone: I can't see a future for myself here either.

Or, instead of accepting the banishment, I wish I had said, of course you can have a future here and I'll help you. We'll fight for it together. You should not have to leave. People need you here, this place needs you. What can I do to help?

But instead of saying that, I promised to get him out of here. We had dreams that were starting to become plans. I had bought three cat carriers for the plane.

25

Dreams

I DROP MY phone on the road and then I kneel on it when trying to retrieve it from a tangle of bedcovers. It causes it to crack and then break more. I hold my phone at an angle and it causes my face to look compressed and I notice how much I look like you. I look more closely. I tilt my phone to get it just right. I really do look like you at around fifteen. I turn to the side. To fulfil my wish, I begin to imagine I am looking at you. Even a beard. Stronger than the beard you had. I feel sad in my heart. So much of you in me. So much of me in you. And I am just looking intently in my dream into my broken phone.

26

Stress After Trauma

THE STRESS after trauma bends and breaks, it inflames joints and makes staircases twice as long and twice as steep. It hangs weights on the body, sends messages of panic through the nerves. It bends and snaps in the brain, raising electric ghosts of the past that flicker like old televisions between channels.

Then again, it's pure love. Your knees, for instance. I see them in the corner of my eye almost continually, the hair of your legs glinting gold in the sun, your forearms, your very soft skin, which I now know to be a sign of the 'genetic variant' that took your life. And the softness between your thumb and finger, I keep seeing that as well.

Sometimes doctors forget and say 'mutation'. The term with the least spin on it would seem to be 'pathological variant' but, even so, I often think that some of the effects of this intrinsic variation in our structural scaffolding have not been pathological. That some of them could even be lovely. In many ways, pathology is undisputed but, in others, a better world would welcome us.

When I go out, I feel exposed on the road like an insect half stuck to asphalt, like a locust. I tell myself I'm merely walking to the shop. I'm walking to the shop because I should. And I should because I've been lying in bed so long, where I feel safe, lying down for so long that my heart is thumping in my ears and standing up makes me dizzy. It is not just walking outside. It is feeling like an insect exposed under the sky, stared at by everyone (there's no one on the street but there will be, any second someone will appear and they will know the horror I saw, they will see it immediately—in such a way I am reliving it), trying to arrange an expression on my face, a non-traumatised and non-traumatic face. By separating myself from the trauma I am reliving it, entering into it, and looking for the exit from inside it, where there is no exit. I am used to mirroring others—but which others now? How to be non-traumatised now? Non-bereaved now? The gulf is too great.

Oh, but there is no choice. They will not have it any other way. The more you move among them the more the tears slowly dry, the fear gets pushed in deeper, the limbs find the patterns of conformity just as they did the first time when you went from crawling towards working.

You know you haven't screamed since you were a child. You don't even know if you can scream. Looking around, it's hard to know if anyone else knows how to scream either.

It is not fine to ask them about it.

I grieved without many friends all this time, but what good friends my son and daughter are to me. Surely, they are better than friends.

They are the best.

It's not a good time to make friends. The stress after trauma is such that sitting in a coffee house and chatting is not permitted.

Official but neglected literature wisely advises the non-bereaved, 'You should run towards the bereaved parent!' It means don't leave them alone. They can't heal alone. They need to feel part of a community. They need people to take them for a walk. Maybe can't walk without another person with them. Maybe can't even cry unless someone touches them.

There are still some things I cannot do, such as return to the scene of the event. My core shakes a little when I see the word for that place. Driving alone is so depressing and used to be even frightening, so I took the kids. Like a small child, many things are frightening and cannot be faced alone. I sleep with cats like they're teddy bears. I even injured my shoulder by cuddling the cat too long in the nook of my arm, cuddling him all night while we both slept. My body became stiff and old and weak. The injury is only just starting to heal after six months. I could not press my seatbelt in and had searing and unbearable pain from putting on a shirt or twirling my scarf across the back of my head. My left arm was redundant and it hurt even while I was sleeping. Of course I thought it was a heart attack.

The stress is deep and sharp. It wounds you and makes you both senescent and childlike. You are scared to go outside. Some are scared to stay inside. My son goes out walking, likes to be seen among non-bereaved, in contexts that look safe and ordinary to him, unlike the swirling confusion of his room in which he is dismantled and his boundaries unclear. Or at least that's what I imagine he is doing. If so, I understand that. It does not occur to me to ask, knowing that we grieve differently, however we grieve. But for me, the amorphous trauma is outside. In my bed I am put together, safe, comfortable and at an even temperature. My room. My writing. Outside, the noises of the world. I'm like Meursault in his cell, hearing the distant steamer's siren, feeling clarity for the last time in the moonlight, waiting for dawn to bring his end. Excuse the spoiler.

The thing no one seems to say: to be stressed after trauma is not only to feel squashed and zapped and shaken. It is not only to avoid reminders of the traumatic event and to be assailed by so-called flashbacks and to relive the events in various ways, to be almost blinded by the past and unable to see what is happening in front of you. It is to be a different person. A person with powerful capacities, like a child, for what adults might call magical or spiritual experiences. It is to be two years old again, or sometimes a more reasonable eight, and sometimes an infant, in a world of nightmares, superstitions and pre-linguistic experiences. Experiences is too clinical a word.

Why can't I be blunt about the trauma that is so blunt with me? To use the language of pragmatic adults, I have visions. Sometimes the visions are stronger than what I see with my eyes. When I found my son, I was literally blinded. Unlike Hamlet, I didn't need to ask my sinews to bear me stiffly up. I did not fall or faint as some do. I was alone, it was around 9 p.m., but it was near the autumnal equinox so it was fully dark. I was alone in a room in which I should not have been alone. The young people like to talk about uncanny valleys on the internet. I know. I raised a few young people and I took an interest as well. The universities like to talk about the *unheimlich* too. Uncanny valleys you have not seen down until you have seen what I saw. When an abyss is he, and you, alone, the crack in reality is too deep and swallows you. It's permanent.

I will tell the truth: I would rather have many heinous crimes committed on my person daily than to stand there in that moment, blinded. And again: many people express more genuine sympathy about a parking fine than the loss of a child.

People are afraid. It's taboo. It's not homely.

I fought back the blackness enough to act. I carved some clinical light out of the heart of it, found a narrow band in which to see and hear and move. Yes, I must have been deafened by trauma's blow too, because I remember my own voice stunted ['It happened. It happened. This is happening'] at the overhead-light-lit white wall of your bedroom corner, everything exposed, over-exposed, over-and-over exposed, and talking into that blindness and carving with voice and eyes a little space in which to continue, in which time could be allowed to keep passing.

But time did not keep passing. Trauma did what poets and prophets do and preferred eternity and the sacred.

I kept trying to find you. I had come to visit, after all.

I will never be the person I was before, but I still remember some of the same stories. I still want to eat and sleep and wear clothing but it's no longer me and I no longer care.

Mystics used to sleep in graves to get this effect. This was the story, which Abu 'Abd ar-Rahman Hatim al-Assam from Balkh (d. 859 AD), told. I used to tell it to my children:

Each morning the devil says to me: What will you wear? What will you eat? And where will you go?

I answer, I will put on a shroud, eat death and dwell in the tomb.

Which is to say, nice try. Which is to say, Matthew 6:25, and the lilies that Jesus said were dressed better than kings, which is true, and the birds that are fed though they labour not …

Time did not keep passing. All the Orientalists and their talk of eternity and the sacred and Mircea Eliade and his eternal return, his cyclic time, all those men who were never mothers, or who were men who lived to age, who must never have looked into that void and heard the world crack, and whose dough clearly wasn't punched down. To them, I say thanks for your thoughts and I don't mean to be rude, but if you could walk to the shops then it's not the same. Because I can't. I can't walk to the shops.

What the psychologists won't acknowledge as they tell you to swivel your eyeballs or tap your knee while 'recalling the traumatic event' so as to free it from its 'traumatic content' (loved one's holy form) or 'somatic involvement' (shaking in your core, nausea, stomach pain like a punch), what they won't tell you is that it's sacred. These memories are the most sacred in my life, too numinous to forget or to remember in full. They are bearing witness to something even more than a birth, which is sacred too, and which many people feel is an important moment in our lives.

These 'intrusive memories', these 're-livings', are my soul swirling around the plughole of Necessity, which is sacred. These trails of memory, these so frightening paths and dwellings inside me that I am never far from (though I can't drive to Footscray), are movements in God's terrifying requiem. It's not his or my personal requiem. It's the world's requiem. When I felt the world crack, it was already that cracked. I just didn't know.

These are my visions and some of their sources and some of the tracks and tremblings in the water as it swirls back again and again towards that frightening blackness. I used to long for that trembling, that stomach pain, again, and move in close to the sheet he died upon, where it hung in my closet in those first weeks, and drawing in close, I would find it again, that shaking in the heart of hearts, the place you never knew before, that communication deeper than my own bones, the extinction, the love that breaks us.

Maybe my son was right, I should have been a Christian.

Eventually, the truth is, we will all lose everything here. We will all lose. Even if he could have lived (to say this, to me, is more exciting than any other prospect in the world), I would have had to part from him. Every person will lose it all. Every one. Every thing. Every every, until you see the plughole I saw.

It's not a syndrome, it's a sacred vision of a usually at least partly hidden reality.

Some never see it until they approach their own death. I got a life sentence.

I carry it with me. It makes Woolworths even harder than usual. And I missed Quiet Hour again by ten minutes. It makes everything here hard. It is, in reality, that hard. This society I live and write in, if you can call it that, really is that hard on people and especially on people who know trauma. On children too, who are not conditioned to it. On people who cannot be conditioned to it. On everyone who isn't directly benefiting from it. The denial of reality in it is what makes it hard.

I can pretend I am not in pain. Is that the aim?

Is there a rung higher, where I stand in awe of Necessity? Is it a degree higher? Really? Handed down from the men in the pulpits of whatever stripe and type? I think not.

It's necessary to get as far as possible from the man on the dais. Not because he's bad or unworthy or whatever. Because he's too far from the void (or some may say, from the cross). Maybe for some men, the closer they get to his feet, that expert at the front of the room, the less worthy they feel themselves, and so that's good for them. For me, the same thing happens in the back row, surrounded by children crying and running, the women chatting and laughing.

Abjection.

It is not polite to discuss religion at the table, and this book is a table. I want you here with me at this table. I don't want you to get up and walk away after just a few bites, making some excuse about how your friend is trying to FaceTime you or that you already ate. I want you here. I know it's not a polite book and I'm not ashamed of that.

There is no way, no way in heaven, hell or this earth that I can talk about this void, this blackening bruising blindness that punched my brain, my stomach, my eyes, my ears, that wrung the clock and the calendar out like a Dali dishcloth, no way I can experience something that has me prefer my eyes skewered, and not talk the language of philosophy and religion sometimes. Weighty enquiry is fine since I feel that heavy anyway. It's the light stuff I can't stand anymore.

Some say it's like carrying a backpack full of bricks that you cannot put down, not even for a second, not even while you're asleep.

And I'm not going to try EMDR, eye movement. I will accept the thousand-mile stare as part of what eyes do when they've seen what I saw.

I am busy, I guess. The mind and heart try to piece the shattered life together, scramble day and night to make a new kind of sense, I guess. It's so exhausting. It feels sometimes like an endless nightmare that you can't wake up from. Some people feel like that.

I only went to group once. A bereaved mother and I stood on the street after. It's like David Foster Wallace said from his 12-step experiences, those platitudes make more sense than anything to us. Keep it simple, stupid. A day at a time.

'Is this yours?' she said, pointing to the car I paused beside.

'Yes, this is me. Is that yours?' I said, pointing to the car a bit further on.

'Yes. That's my car.'

'It's not long for us, you know,' she said. 'It's only eight months. I think we are still in shock.'

'I think so. Yes. I think we are still in shock.'

'And I think I'm fine, you know. I'm doing well. But then I think I am actually deeply, deeply depressed without even knowing it.'

'I wonder about that, too. I think I am very deeply depressed and I don't know it.'

'I think we are both in deep depression but somehow functioning all the time.'

'And then I think that I am functioning all the time and have been doing well but I remember I have spent many months in bed. And maybe I am still in bed a lot. I don't remember.'

We repeat ourselves a lot and talk very slowly. Finding our cars was difficult.

I am in bed now writing this. It is noon. Should I be keeping track of how much I am in bed? I put on fifteen kilos or more, I don't know. But I'm a product of this place here, and so I much prefer the romantic idea of being gaunt, the ghoulish feminine melancholic. Unlike the rugged male counterpart, melancholia diminishes her body and she wastes away, while he tends to somehow stay in shape as if someone is secretly feeding him porridge and encouraging him to work out while he broods. It seems more seemly to become gaunt, and it would be easier to fit into my clothes. And I think how awful that I have increased in biological existence and worldly mass when he … But I know that's part of the whole point of expanding from a tenuous point that floats in the doona in the semi-dark of the womb, I mean room—I am trying to keep an anchor here. To be a child again, to be scared and be a child. My body becomes a parent, puts me to bed, weighs me down with food, makes me stay home and rest. Makes me heavy, makes me grow in such a way as I can't decide if I am descending slowly into the mass of the earth, approaching my death (it's not acceptable to harm myself, so, if so, it should be averted—I am thinking of buying an electronic Walking Pad for my bedroom), or if I'm just trying to stay in bed more because I'm tired.

There is a little more to say about stress after trauma, a syndrome. I really am too tired now.

27

Highest Heaven

IN DREAMS, you can't turn on the light. Your dreams' brightness setting is already the maximum energy you have. There is no artificial lighting in a dream. In the same way, you cannot imagine heaven.

In one of my communities, if a person's close one has departed, people will say, *Grant him jannatul firdaus.* May God grant him the highest heaven. Jannah is garden. Firdaus is *pardis*, *paradeisos*, a walled garden, the garden of Eden, Paradise. Parks and gardens on high. I'm not looking into it. I'm trying to see it.

How can you turn on the light? How can you produce more brightness and more happiness than you already know. You can't.

My mind can't climb up, can't reach.

When my son said he was about to enrol in horticulture, I think it was during our last conversation. I had an immediate and (it turns out) permanent image of what it would be like. It was unrealistic in this life but I think it was real in eternity.

I realised that I shouldn't do a job that involves too much interaction. I think the solitude would be good. I think I could do it.

I don't know what we said. Something like this.

I think it's perfect.

And I saw the vast grassy slope, so fresh and green, stretching up from where my mind's eye went, in some imaginary idyllic botanic garden. He was on a quiet ride-on mower—it probably made no sound at all—tending peacefully the grassy slopes, happily employed.

A vision.

Now I cling to that.

It's the best paradise I could imagine here or anywhere.

Hereafter, we say.

Here but after. Here but not now.

It made me think.

At first a heaven is different from here. It's so much better. There is no pain, no filth, no stool, no menses. To take a negative path to it, it's obvious what won't be there. I remember him with all his flaws and me with about a thousand more because I had more time to cultivate them, to backslide, to dwell in myself. The best flight is from your faults. He took flight. He was bewildered, but then he shook, he suddenly flew over the slopes and went between trees somewhere I couldn't follow and into the sky.

And into the earth.

And the space in between that my body now tries to bridge.

There is a rainbow between the two, and a dove.

The highest heaven was when I was rubbing aloe vera on his feet when he was two or three years old and woke in the night with itchy feet.

The highest heaven was when I breastfed him until he was two.

It was when I heard the doorbell when he was fifteen, sixteen, seventeen, the way he pressed and held it for suspense for a hilariously long time, diiiiiiiiiiiiiiiiiiiiiiiiiiiiiiing dong.

So that I would know it was him. We never discussed it.

I loved it.

And the way when I opened the door my arms would fly up from my sides automatically, from joy.

Woot! I would exclaim, childish, regaining sight, regaining hearing, whole in your presence.

There was no greater miracle, no greater heaven, than you, here, alive, with me, my child. That was the secret of it all.

Yet now, without that, I must find a way across the valley myself, my arms at my sides, cubits of earth in my own chest.

I love you.

There are too many subjects in that sentence to carry across the valley. Two of them have to go.

I. You.

Then I realised it. Maybe we don't have to go. I don't know what heaven is, the grassy slopes of the other side, idyllic labour, secure employment, companions of equal age and a full cup. I'm just not sure. I haven't had enough delights—other than the delight of sharing life with my children—to know what otherworldly delights might be like, if they were more of the same. We didn't know about it. And that's how

I realised it: heaven might be obscure to me, but the *highest* heaven, it must be exactly exactly exactly like this.

Like this.

The higher you go, the closer you get to the ground. *Do not transport bodies to their country of birth. To be buried in the dirt, anywhere on Earth, is to be buried in gold.*

When I go I may find myself here—here—with the worst behind us.

Outside my window now, there is the sweetest pink luminosity across a band of soft grey cloud. Pale pink flare. The name of a prescient story I wrote about you. (Imagine if what we had was enough? Oh, you are the one I want to ask about it!)

And the pale pink flare in my breast tells me that what I did was maybe even enough.

I mean—!!

Enough!

Imagine that.

It was a story about you leaving.

… *I think of him breathing, breathing like nobody breathes anymore, and sighing into the morning sky—for some reason, where he is it's morning and there's strong sunshine—and rising from the rocks, slamming the back door and moving down the outside of the house, holding the wall, feeling his way along the bricks* …

It was a story about you rising from the back step and walking away like a wounded giant who realises, at last, that he is not a giant and not even wounded, *walking not because there is anywhere to go, because there isn't anywhere, but to find out about walking.*

I never knew that story was about this. It was about this. Much writing is prescient, which begs the question, 'What is writing?'

I emailed that story to you. I remember thinking 'Don't email it, why don't you print it out and give it to him, or wait till you publish it, or wait till you see him next and …' but that voice, the very quiet voice but that same voice said, 'Do it now. Email it to him. There might not be another chance.' That voice is to be obeyed. I emailed it. I was so moved that you wept when you read it.

We talked about it on the phone.

I didn't ask enough questions.

But I said thank you a lot of times, and I said, that means a lot to me. Thank God for that.

*Next step: renounce feet.** The sun has set in the west, at your feet, out my window, in my heart.

Here.

It's going to be right here and you're going to be you.

---

* Jalāl al-Dīn Muhammad Balkhī (d. 1273).

28

Meursault

HOW MUCH should I care about Meursault? A lot, I think.

Meursault, of course, is a character written by Camus. It is obvious to me that the book Meursault would write would be very different. And yet it is such a true book. There are moments Camus comes in and moments he moves out to make space for Meursault. I'm grateful for him making that space for someone like Meursault, who I consider part of my invisible community. For me, Meursault was a good friend who I could not have met any other way. I often forget the central plot point. I have often spent time in the cell with him alone on the last night on Earth, wishing everyone would just finally hate us more vigorously. I am tired of it.

Camus based the character of Meursault closely on his 'eccentric' friend. It has been obvious to me that Meursault is something like me and my family members. I certainly can't think when the sun glints off things and I wouldn't know whether or not to drink milk coffee at a vigil either.

I remember many times hearing my first son's voice, in just the same tone as Meursault's, informing me of things. I was never shocked. I never thought it meant he lacked empathy. I once went for a short break from my newborn, to stretch my legs and get some air. I wasn't far away. My literal-minded first-born son located me and informed his mother (that's me) in a flat tone, without the slightest alarm, 'The baby is lying there saying wah-hu wah-hu wah-hu.' Not knowing what it meant, he simply provided me with an imitation. He didn't know what the baby meant by it but he must have felt that I would be better placed to understand and respond, so he simply informed me. I was very grateful. I appreciated that style of communication, so free from interpretation. When I went inside, I found that he was one hundred per cent right. The baby was saying *wah-hu, wah-hu, wah-hu*, in those distressed cry-hiccups of newborns. The word crying must not have seemed apt. The distress did not communicate itself to my son. I am not sure if it communicated itself to me either. Love did. Love knew. But I was never a mother who knew what people meant when they said, 'You will soon learn to interpret his cries.' I did not learn to interpret his cries or anything else.

Interpreting and responding are two different things.

It was in that same tone that my same son came to me a year and a half later, as I have mentioned, when I had stepped out of the bathroom and he had called out loudly enough but without any alarm, 'The baby is under the water.'

Some might interpret that as a detachment. Those people would be one hundred per cent wrong. I've been told I value rightness and wrongness too highly. I have been told that is part of my condition. I have been told that people like us have a communication deficit. That's an interpretation. It does not give reliable information.

When my son grew up and stopped saying *wah-hu* when anyone could hear and learnt not to slip down into the water, he said to me, 'It's all rubbish. You are not ill. You do not have a syndrome or a disease or a deficit. That's how they get you. Mental shackles.'

He was one hundred per cent right.

He also said, 'You'll never get better, no one will ever understand, and life will always be impossible.'

Right again.

My older son informed me of something else too. It was a definition of autism, which he forwarded me: *Different things may be obvious to me than you.*

A deficit of empathy is one of the most perplexing mistakes made by those who would see the problem as one-sided. How bewildering it is to me as someone who, just like my son, spent my life trusting everyone, who was the first to stop and help someone, to get cash from the ATM for a stranger, to put my life in danger to pick up male hitchhikers in rural areas, to let homeless people live in my house, to raise my three kids when their fathers didn't stay, to take dead animals off the road and give them decent burials.

Just last week I stopped at the side of the highway in case a rainbow lorikeet wasn't as dead or broken as it looked. After we flew over the top of it in the car, I saw in my rear-view mirror its wing, raked up by the wind. A mock wave.

'What are you doing, Mum,' my daughter said, 'It's dead.'

Maybe not! Maybe not!

I ran back and found it trying to sit up to see me. I threw a cushion cover, which unfortunately had cat pee on it, over its head. It was the only cloth in my car, in the boot awaiting a laundromat trip that might never happen. I carried the bird from the boiling asphalt to the trees. A man was mowing, it was loud, so I took it to the other side of the highway but there was a sharp drop into the valley. The base of the gum tree looked sparse and hot with curled bark and twigs. I unwrapped the bird's talons from where it held on to my finger like a baby's tiny hand holds a finger and transferred it to the grass. It looked at me drunkenly. Different things were obvious to us perhaps.

It's alive! What do we have to hold water in in this car? A dish, anything?

We had just bought some pens. My daughter suggested opening the packet and using the bubble plastic. Carried the spring water and packaging across the road.

The bird was sitting up, hot, beak open, watching the approach.

Seeing my form enlarging and closing the distance between us, something trembled about it, something about it shook to life, it puffed itself out like a new butterfly and took off from the edge of the mountain, letting out a single loud squawk, swooping down into the valley and then rising, rising and away into treetops!

When I read about *L'Étranger*, I am so shocked when they say 'who refuses to comply to society's norms' and 'without the capacity for empathy'. What?

I think Camus must have liked his eccentric friend very much. I don't get the sense he just unempathetically used him for material. Though I haven't considered Camus' empathy one way or the other.

I wonder how he knew that sometimes we just wish everyone would properly hate us. That's quite a deep secret, I thought.

How life can come undone from all the good-willed little things you did to fit in, like a café au lait at the vigil (which, let us remember, had not technically started yet), or a cigarette at the vigil, which you politely accept, or like not faking more commitment than you felt. Mirroring people but not noticing that your performance was being judged or knowing for what it was judged. Not being able to do the double take of knowing how they see you. Not believing that they really were so different from you because you were unable to see yourself from the outside.

And later, they remember. It all comes out. You are not right. There is something wrong with you. Different things were obvious to you.

They say trauma and autism look similar. The ego punched down like bread dough. Not knowing how to care about the self or know what is meant by self. Failing to be sophisticated enough to produce adequate levels of hypocrisy.

They say that the good shepherd will go into the valley even after his one lost sheep. He will leave the rest of the flock behind and go searching in the night until he finds him and bring him back into the fold from wherever he has strayed.

The opposite of forcing conformity. I wish there were more people doing that.

I sometimes hear the distant steamship's siren and know that the affairs of the world no longer concern me, if they ever did. Rainbow lorikeets still do. It is obvious to me that there are so, so many unfortunate people locked outside where I am sitting, peacefully, in beatitude even, in this cell, in the window's moonlight, with my departed son, with fictional Meursault, alone.

29

Finding or Finding Out

THERE IS a difference. No one speaks of it. Even in bereavement circles, I can't get any traction on this question.

I tried to invite those with a similar experience to this question. If I make too many qualifications, it's too wordy and no one even knows what I'm asking. If I don't, I'm so blunt that I could shock already fragile people.

And then again, this is how it always is, like the old story of the donkey and the mother and her son. They pass through many towns on their travels and each time they see someone, a new criticism is brought, in response to their adjustment to the last critique of their behaviour.

Why are you riding that donkey, Mother, while your son, younger and weaker, is forced to walk alongside?

Mother, why do you spoil that boy by letting him ride while you, his elder, are forced to trudge?

Oh, look at that Mother and son forcing that poor donkey to carry both of them when one of them could easily walk alongside or take turns!

Ah, look how foolish those two are, carrying their donkey on their heads instead of letting it carry them!

All possible combinations of words and actions will draw criticism. I read that story when I was under ten. Why have I still not understood?

It comes as the biggest shock imaginable to all of us, I wrote, unsure of whose voice I was imitating (probably an amalgam of familiar voices—we all imitate each other to be safe; occasionally someone strikes out and says something idiosyncratic, challenging and shocking—but the last thing any of us needs is more of a shock), *no matter how we find out, whether from a long illness or in a sudden, unexpected way, nothing can change the fact that they are gone.*

Whose voice is this? Honestly.

Now for the difficult part. *Some of you have had the terrible experience of being with your children when they passed or hearing the news. I cannot imagine what that must have felt like, but I imagine it would make you feel beyond powerless, beyond desperate.*

I cannot get to my point.

Now the even more difficult part. *Many of us experience symptoms of post-traumatic stress. It is traumatic for all of us. I am having a lot of flashbacks, sometimes almost constantly, to the moments and circumstances. I was alone, it was dark outside, it was sudden and terrifying. I went there to see someone I had known for almost twenty years, as close to me as anyone else on Earth—*

Get to the point. *If it was like this for you, how did you deal with the traumatic stress and shock? (which I think gets in the way of grieving and I've always thought so, even though an early counsellor said that 'we don't pathologise grief this early'). I thought we could at least talk about it together maybe.*

Too wordy. It won't work.

It didn't.

Replies only from those whose replies started with, *I didn't find my child, but …*

But I was desperate to know I wasn't alone, desperate to hear from those who had. I still am.

I want to talk about it with someone who knows. (An early counsellor, dismissively, called it 'peer support' and told me not to rely on it.)

No pre-mortem diagnosis, no phone calls or updates, no hospital, no ambulance, no knock at the door, no decisions, no plans.

Some came close. Some, after phones were not answered, went to visit and found the door locked. They called the police. They never saw what was inside.

I feel I've seen the inside of the kernel of the fruit of God's Earth.

The void in there that somehow would become life.

Now that I have seen inside, I know that the seed cannot sprout.

I am cracked.

Not even.

What-was-I cracked.

Where are the others?

One of the differences that bereaved parents mention is that waking up is the worst. When they wake up, they have forgotten and then suddenly it floods back. I understand the concept, but it never happened to me. My body always knew, my mind always knew, all through the night, enduringly. There was never a time when I didn't know. A son-shaped pattern inside me was formed by the invisible axe, chipped off the edge of the trillion cells that know him. Even in dreams, I knew.

That is not to say that it was small enough to know in the usual way. I couldn't know it, not really. I still can't and I hope I never will. I am known by it. I am grasped in the invisible fist all the time. It squeezes away anything not the shape of my son. It wrings me out.

There are a few camps. I am from the Enduring Bonds camp, not the Denial is the First Phase camp.

The shock of finding led to severe physical effects that meant the event could not be forgotten, not for a second.

It was not an absence declared. It was a presence discovered. Within his room and within me. Him. He. A breath escaping. It's not hyperbole.

It would be easier not to discuss it, theoretically, but easier no longer has much meaning. Only avoiding further trauma has meaning.

When that physical agony, for relief from which any of us would exchange severe toothache, for relief from which many would exchange four limbs, in place of which most of us would prefer terminal diagnoses or any number of other things we used to fear, including death—when that physical agony of the finding shock started to wane, I was frightened. It was my anchor. There was the pain and the grave, the only two things that caused me to know for certain that I no longer lived in the same world.

A caterpillar gets time to digest itself. There was no time. It happened in a split second. Seconds wrestled with Time, shunting on rails trying to gain ground, slipping back in shards and breaks and clattering. I couldn't hear my voice. I couldn't see.

Even when I peered into your face, I couldn't see.

I couldn't kneel. I couldn't take a relaxed posture. I had to stay up. I couldn't kneel down to touch your head with my right hand, only stoop a little to touch with my left. There were strict rules in Necessity. Blinking was not good, closing my eyes forbidden.

The policeman didn't know there were rules. He didn't know that sitting down on your weights bench was offensive. That it had become sacred. He was kind enough. But he was not under the hammer blow of Necessity and the weights were from different measures.

They say one day you will not think so much about the time and way of their passing but remember happy times.

Sometimes I don't relate to the ones who found out. I didn't find out except by finding and it's different. There are sudden shocks that flick your cells off, twinkle them and snuff them out. I could die from that shock. And I knew that if I didn't care if I did, it was more likely. I tried to care for the sake of my other children.

If I had a dollar for every bereaved parent who gets a serious illness within two years …

Grief is exhausting. Trauma is exhausting. Try to take care of yourself.

A caterpillar gets plenty of time to prepare the cocoon and digest itself. It has time to find the right leaf, to rest and find the one part of its body that can be relied on to survive the transmutation. Then it knows it can let go of everything else. That small part will be the basis of building the new form. It's an intricate and precise matter.

This is also an intricate and precise matter. It also takes a long time. But all of it has to be done after the fact.

It's true, I think this: if only I could have died with you, if only you hadn't been alone and then I hadn't been alone.

I love you. I said there are two too many subjects involved in that now. You've done your part. It is I who cannot catch up to myself or ever will again because I was too late.

There was no goodbye, only my turning to you at the bus stop in Footscray, after you told me how to walk to the train station, so that I could return home, and you could return to your flat and your government-mandated online Certificate II in Retail.

Go all the way along this road until you reach the tram tracks and then turn right.

The sight of the bus turning the corner and coming towards us, herald of our parting.

The first hug—

I love you.

The second hug—

See you soon, and I turned away. I felt so secure, so unbewildered, following your perfect directions, as if you were right there walking with me.

30

A Day or Part of a Day

EVERY FRIDAY we are meant to read the ancient story of the youths who betook themselves to the cave. Their world was a mess. The people were all evil. These were Christian youths and righteous, good people. So they betook themselves to a cave and withdrew from their society. The story is very old. It has landed in the Quran at the middle point, as if there is a cave in the middle of the Quran as well. Every Friday we are meant to re-read it, or recite it if we remember.

I remember there is confusion about the number of youths but it doesn't matter. The point is that they slept there in the cave, with a dog, and the stars turned and the moon rose and set outside the mouth of the cave.

You would have seen …

They turn from one side to another, sleeping.

Then, when they wake up, they ask each other how much time has passed and they say, perhaps a day or part of a day.

They decide that one of them should go down into the valley to buy food from the town. But when they get there, the population is transformed and everyone is Christian. When they take out their coins to pay, the seller turns pale with fear. There is a different ruler on the coins now. The youths are trying to pay with ancient coins. It has been hundreds of years since they betook themselves to the cave. Now the people are righteous like the youths. But the youths become afraid for their lives because they cannot explain what has happened. So they hide their coins and try to disguise the miracle, but people find out, and after some time they put a plaque outside the cave to commemorate the miracle. And you can look up the plaque and the cave now on the internet. It's very famous.

The story of the cave is important to people because they believe it has a deep meaning.

It has three meanings to me that I've been able to notice. One, that if you can't change the state of things and things have gone evil, you can at least withdraw from it. Two, sometimes doing nothing is better. Three, time is not what it seems.

Now a fourth, and I hope it can be a tradition that continues: when I go to the graveyard, fortnightly or weekly, I am visiting my sleeping Christian youth in his cave. I know that he lies there and the stars turn and the moon rises and sets. I see by the condition of other graves that time has passed in that graveyard. More than a hundred years and those sleepers are still sleeping, and the world out here still has the same coins as when my son withdrew to the cave. So far everyone has not become righteous. I know he was right and the world is full of evil. I do not know what world he will wake to.

If you think about your child sleeping for a hundred years or more, while regimes change and populations change and while no one they knew still lives on this earth anymore, it is very lonely.

Some say that the cave is the heart and that a good person should withdraw to the cave of their heart and be as if sleeping. Some say you should die before you die.

That advice is lost on my son. It is lost on me. It is just something some people like to say.

All I know is that I have withdrawn to the cave and it is a different cave from my son's. I am not sleeping well. Each day, while the stars turn and the moon rises and sets outside my window, I turn from one side to the other; my neck becomes more and more painful from weakness or from lying in bed too much (I'm in bed now, again), or stress from time passing and the world still being evil.

Time seems to pass in increments, like a second hand jolting on an old clock. I feel it. I make a hollow beneath my ear so that I cannot hear my heartbeat through my pillow. Time is marked by visits to the grave where he waits. Weeks, fortnights, months pass and soon, a year will pass. Then years will be marked off, punctuated by visits to the cave, to the grave. Fridays will come and go and come and go and come and go. I will forget to read 'The Cave' on many of them, and this series of forgettings and non-markings will be marked by occasional rememberings.

Today is Saturday and I'm late by a day, just as I was late by a day or part of a day, or, God help me, more than that.

The way I mark time by going to the grave, and the way he marks time by his stillness and silence and his commitment to resting there, and the way the world goes on around us, presumably heading for a change of ruler or a sudden appearance of Jesus in clouds of glory, or a gentle awakening such as yours in my dream, looking up at me so, so, so sleepy you were—and you said thickly, hulllllooo Mama! as you always did, with your so beautiful sleepy face, and I knew you were waking from the realisation that you had passed away, that your sleep had been too deep, and in my dream I saw you rising out of it to greet me on the other side of the event.

I didn't ask you how long you had slept and you didn't ask me. You were dizzy when you stood up. You were tall and thin. Then you went to have a shower and your bed was empty. I realised, hearing the sound of the shower from the other room, that you weren't coming back into the room. I realised that the police would be along soon and they'd arrive and find no body. That I'd better get out of here. They are not going to like it. They won't understand.

So when I punctuate time like this, leaping from grave visit to grave visit, from mornings with stiff necks to mornings with stiff necks, to my period, from Friday to Friday, from semester to September teaching the youths, from Christmas to Christmas, Ramadan to Ramadan, Easter to Easter, there is also a long stretching out of unmarkable time from the moment when the axe came down and broke me, and when the wild and irregular beating and silences of your heart in deep sleep (was that what happened?), which broke you from the mooring of your body on your bed, and this long unremarkable time stretches out and cannot be marked by anything.

My breaths, my own heart, they are just parts of a clock running down now, running down, slowing down, enlivened hardly at all by those injections of funds into my bank every fortnight, or those emails that rise to the surface of the phone, alerts or those regular and irregular interruptions from the world. Like the lifetimes of the cats that still live here with me, in our warm and temporary fluffy comforting life. I know that the timer has been set. Time is running out. And it is going to run out slowly and painfully, it is going to run out as the cats pass away, as me or the other children in whatever order are passing away, as all the people on this earth pass away. And your grave will be there, the moon will rise and fall, the stars will turn.

Even if I live for a short time after you, it will be long because it is a long time to note that your child is not breathing. To note them not breathing for an hour, a day, a month, nine months, a year, and I do not think past that. These mentionings and notings and markings are all the stars that turn and the moon that rises and falls. In reality, I too am in the cave. I am writing this from a deep sleep.

It is frightening to think of a thousand years passing on this earth and you still lonely there without my visits. No one will come. It's a short walk from where I park the car and on the way it's possible to see all of these outcomes.

Seamus Heaney said that perhaps we should each think of our own unmarked grave and start from there.

I avoid falling into the trap of monuments that can collapse. One of my communities is right. Let it be earth so that vegetation can grow. Living vegetation will remember God on the deceased's behalf. Even if no one comes. I look at images of Simone Weil's grave for inspo.

When I think of that thousand years, my own living, breathing, pulsing life that I have left seems short and, from such a distance in time, I can almost imagine that we passed away at the same time. The graveyard sees it that way. There are generations but all are together.

I am not a sociopath but I get daily comfort from looking at the people who pass me in streams in the street, and thinking, 'In one hundred years, we'll all be dead.'

Yet, feeling all this passing time, hours and hours and days and days and months and months when I haven't run to you, haven't joined you, I pray that the waiting is not hard for you. No one wants to wait in a grave or in a cave or a prison. One must rest there.

This morning I read Kafka's 'The Knock at the Manor Gate'. It tells of large leaps through time that are like the leaps I've done in my dreams, the semi-flying absurd leaps that cover a lot of ground (in waking life I have short legs and cannot even keep up with ordinary walkers). In 'The Knock at the Manor Gate' the events of a single day, a short walk, and a page and a half, span a lifetime. A boy, walking home with his sister, progresses through a trial and his long imprisonment in a dungeon. It begins with 'It was summer, a hot day. With my sister I was passing the gate of a great house on our way home.' The silly knock his sister does or pretends to do on the gate of the manor house results in persecution and a legal affair that proceeds apace. Without any signal or warning, the clock has been recalibrated. A second equals perhaps a decade and then the difference increases exponentially until time bends backwards so that, at the end, he wonders, 'Could I still endure any air other than prison air? That is the great question, or at least it would be, if I still had any prospect of release.'

I pray every day for my young sleeper, 'Let it be only a day or part of a day—'

Time is never more exhausting than it feels on the waking heart. The night passes in an instant. An age could pass like that.

For me also, can it be that a time will come when I will look back and think that the distance between losing him and finding him again (all those grave visits and years collapsing together), will just seem like a day or part of a day?

Is the rest of my life long enough to do one or two things, just like a day is?

At the end of an hour, you remember three things; at the end of a day, you remember three things; at the end of a life, three things …

Unless something comes to knock out one of the major three things of my life, I am already at the end of my life in that regard. I already know the three things I will remember.

Swirling like this, like stars around Necessity, around the miracle. All else spinning off into oblivion. There are stories of caves and also stories of spindles. Cycles of time. Weaving and rending. Remembering, remembering and remembering.

31

Men

THE NUMBER of men I trust and love in this world is now reduced by drastic half. From two to one. Both of them grew in my womb. One of them is now separated from me by some earth and an unknown span of time. And both reside within and have their home here with me, as well as wherever they find themselves to be. I do not have access to their minds, but we are cut from the same cloth. *Every tree has a fruit and the fruit of the heart is your child.* Abu'l-Qasim Muhammad ibn Abdullah (d. 632) said this and, later, Elizabeth Stone said that *to have a child is to have your heart go walking around outside your body*, or, in my case, to shovel dirt on top of your heart and have to walk away. And then to keep walking around. Stone's formula is popular but the older one has a seed and doesn't leave me hollowed out and heart-less in this life. I'm being literal-minded maybe. *Burial rites are the oldest known human practice,* etc. *Lay her i' th' earth/And from her fair and unpolluted flesh/may violets spring!*, etc.

I still love and trust the one who went, as much as before or more, but he is not in this world in the same way as he was before. I want to hear his take on things, ask him how to get to the train station, be safe with him, walk with him into the new world that existed with him and now without him.

You found two men to trust too, my son.

You found Kafka and soon felt sorry for him but only through a mutual understanding. And last night, Christmas night, I dreamt of the other one you found, I dreamt of your pastor. I was hugging him.

Kafka said, you are the knife I twist inside myself—this is love. When I read that, via the pain in my heart more than via thought, I thought of you immediately.

32

Do You Want to Run?

DIFFERENT THINGS are obvious to me than to the makers of *Love on the Spectrum*. Maybe that's because most of the people with my views—that we are all in an inhumane experimentation lab, some more than others—wouldn't watch a curated set of autistic people go on curated dates. But I watch a lot of things that I wouldn't watch. With my laptop propped sideways on my bed, I watch a societally disabled minority receive training, on camera, on how to interact as if they are not autistic in order to meet other people who are autistic.

Would you like some tea?

Oh yes please. That would be wonderful.

I want you to know that I have very much enjoyed this evening.

Oh thank you. I have also enjoyed myself.

I watch people undergo training sessions in how to be having different urges than the ones they are having. If the people on this show feel like jumping up from the dinner date because it's boring and going for a quick run outside in the fresh air, they will not be able to do so.

To successfully meet with another person, they will have to sit still and grimace and say, 'Oh really. How interesting. Do you have any other hobbies?' because they have been told that this is the right way to get to know another person, especially with a view to intimacy.

To make a connection with another person, you must suppress your nature and put a false and generic nature in its place. Compensation will be made afterwards, via the receipt of approval as a deposit and love if paid in full. It is a transaction. A bargain.

Bereaved people discuss social occasions in similar ways. A convincing performance is required. It is up to you to bridge the gap.

Since my son went, the thousand-mile stare through the screen sometimes catches on background details. I watch whole movies looking at the plants and clouds in them. I watch entire series noticing lamps. Or, in this case, sadistic filming techniques and wardrobing decisions.

At times, in the restaurant, the camera pans conspiratorially past the autistic daters to the tables of other couples, who are clinking glasses naturally or laughing and chatting in an immersed kind of way. There are times when the camera pans over the bodies of the autistic subjects as well, careful to reveal the incorrect number of times the woman plays with her hair like a little girl, or how the man folds his napkin in despair.

Is it a masking contest?

The dating pairs have been dressed in similar clothes, perhaps to trick them into feeling they belong together. A man in a salmon pink polo shirt will be paired with a woman in a salmon pink jacket. Vegetative themes on a shirt are mirrored on a dress and in a leafy setting for the date, almost as though they have been forced to harmonise with their environment, in imposed camouflage, forced to conform to each other and a certain habitat.

It's almost as though there might be a place for them, for us, in the uncomfortable world others built, that suits hardly any species of animal or any type of person on earth but suits some far better than others. They are dressed up this way and coached in what to say 'to keep the conversation going', whether they enjoy that conversation or not.

They are taught to feign interest in something for which they have none, and a happiness that they do not feel. That's what a date is.

After the awkward goodbye, in which a woman struggles to decide how many thank yous is enough, we watch as she almost trips on the unsteadiness of the moment. When she leaves the restaurant, the camera lingers on the lower half of her body as she walks away, exhibiting to us her unique gait and the way the black heels she has been dressed up in for the night, paired perfectly with the black dress, are almost impossible for her. She teeters like a girl in a woman's clothes, like a girl in a woman's body, at first, but it's a trick of the camera—really, she teeters like a person in other people's decisions, like a person in an autistic woman's life in a reality television show in which she is not getting paid. Just act naturally. And wear these. And sit here. And say that.

But this teetering, the camera teaches us, is just her. It is nothing to do with the fact that the entire system of being a woman is absolutely untenable for every single woman, though for some more than others, no matter how highly trained their walking and talking and glass-clinking styles. And for every man too, I vehemently assume. How can anyone live in this world? This woman's body is a chink of light through the broken artefact we were born in, a ray of hope. To me. That's what's very obvious to me.

If only more people found more difficult things so difficult that they couldn't hide it.

Love is a miracle, the dearest dream, a symbol of all our hopes, and all we want is to love and be loved forever and for our hearts to be joined for eternity. It would be amazing to find true love. This is what the people on the show say when they are asked about it. But when one woman is asked the same question by her date, who is following his script, she replies, Oh anything really. Anything at all. Anyone. I don't really mind.

Perhaps it hasn't occurred to her to feign an ability to imagine the existence of another person. Perhaps she cannot imagine how many others think that they can imagine the existence of another person when, in reality, they can't.

She hadn't been coached out of Simone Weil's opinion: *It is given to very few minds to discover that things and beings exist.*

This show puts forward that you should act like you know about the existence of yourself and others even if you don't.

Most don't, but they have mastered the act. She too is generally quite good at faking it, but her comment lays things bare.

My son and I always responded well when we saw human beings making genuine and direct communications about their pain or their exuberance. Emergencies did not scare us. But dinner dates and formal social occasions were off the table.

I have only had to sit through a few dinner dates in my life. One I thoroughly enjoyed because it had not yet occurred to me that I should hide my nature. I sat cross-legged and barefoot on the seat and had a wonderful time chatting with this man after his workday. I thought he looked very nice in his shirt. It was not obvious to me what all the other people in there were doing or thinking, or what was going on around me. I learnt to use chopsticks. He paid. He was nice. I felt very grown up.

The opposite happened decades later. He had run through lists of things that I might be interested in doing with him on the weekend and had given me 'options'. There had been many weeks like that. I had not known how to say that I cannot imagine any future time. And I don't have social interests or preferences that involve others. And my health is not good. There are many days when I do not leave my room.

Decades without enough health, money or babysitters (without any babysitters) also contributed to future plans and weekends being things that other people do.

After he sent the main options, there would be sub-options of which movie, which dinner, and I would be expected to choose or express my preferences on things I had no preference on, as well as to be grateful for the options. Then there would be more sub-options like a preference for Friday night or Saturday night and where to meet and when. I wanted to jump out of my skin. He did all of this perfunctorily, as though following an instruction manual.

So, on the date, we were sitting at a table by the window and we were now deeply involved in sub-sub-sub-sub options of what type of food I might like. I became more glum, exhausted, bored, alienated and disturbed. He performed vigilance and responsiveness to the minutest detail. I had not found a way to communicate anything. By this time, I felt like a germ in a Petri dish being ministered to by a focused pathologist.

When Kafka was asked how his engagement party went, he said he felt tied hand and foot like a prisoner. That's how I felt at the table by the window too. We were in mid-conversation, people were strolling by outside the window in the night, my clothes were quite comfortable, which is always a big factor, and I wasn't aware of any particularly high anxiety. Somewhere out there were my son, my son and my daughter, and I was whole and still imagining I could somehow hold life together.

I was mid-sentence when I suddenly felt total disorientation and lost my ability to talk. He didn't notice. He kept on talking. The reason I couldn't speak anymore was that I didn't recognise him. He looked like a total stranger to me. I felt fear. I told myself what his name was, tried to reassure myself, but the name didn't sound right either. I told myself that the experience, whatever it was, would wear off.

That experience did not wear off. I recovered my ability to say the right things like 'Yes, it has been lovely. I suppose we should be heading off. No, I don't want dessert, what about you?' And he didn't notice or, if he did, I couldn't notice him noticing. But the sense of him being a stranger never went away.

It was the opposite of bonding, when you feel someone is so familiar they might as well be you, like the way I feel about my children. They are a part of you, you are part of them and that much, at least, can be taken for granted. This was like encountering an enemy species. I never found a way to put it into words, and I still haven't, not quite. When I told my son about it, he just nodded emphatically.

After Kafka met the woman he would soon propose to, he wrote in his diary: 'I was not at all curious about who she was, but rather took her for granted at once. Bony, empty face that wore its emptiness openly. Bare throat. A blouse thrown on … . (I alienate myself from her a little by inspecting her so closely …) Almost broken nose. Blonde, somewhat straight, unattractive hair, strong chin.' This is love, to assume someone exists, to see an emptiness that doesn't hide. Unattractive hair. What a relief. No masks.

A hundred years later, Kafka's love letters are unaccountably laid on the Petri dish. They are found to be Kafkaesque.

I hesitate to analyse my experience in the restaurant. There are many things it could be about (a metaphor for my alienation) or it could be literal: I felt like we didn't know each other because we didn't know each other.

It also happened in the place that I can no longer go to, one of the places on trauma's map that is too tangled and frightening. I was looking out the window to the street where that bus stop is, or connected to it, but I don't quite know where it is. My map is in pieces inside me, I can't find the connections and I'm scared to make them even if I could. It was as if I sensed that soon my current life and my current self would be suddenly emptied out. Whatever happiness there could have been that summer wasn't meant for that me or for that time at all, it was just to store up a small amount of resources for what was coming. Something in me had reached a limit and a faint voice was saying, 'Installation complete. Do you want to run?'

33

Sweet Fresh Wind off the Sea

I DON'T KNOW if this is appropriate.

It's hard to protect my privacy or my son's privacy and that matters to me quite a lot. Telling the truth about grief, about life, also matters.

Let your gaze not be studious, let it not be invasive. Do not study me as I limp. The limping is not of any interest. Disclaimer. You and everyone you know will die. You and everyone you know will suffer. You and everyone you know will limp like this and will become limp. If you are not disabled now, you will be. You will cry, you will mourn and you will go where my son went. You may or may not get the chance to suffer as much. There is also Simone Weil's 'terrible prayer'.* I never got the chance to ask you what you think of it.

An example of a prayer, she writes in her notebook. *Father, in the name of Christ grant me this. That I be unable to will any bodily*

* Some say Weil's prayer is terrible but is it not just a version of Luke 14:11?— 'whosoever exalteth himself shall be abased; and he that humbleth himself shall be exalted.' It sounds to me like a prayer for everlasting life.

movement … That I be incapable of receiving any sensation … That I be unable to make the slightest connection between two thoughts …

Suffering is what it is. It is insight. It is affliction. And whatever else suffering may be, it is not for your viewing pleasure unless there is something wrong with you.

Now that we've got that out of the way let me plunge back into innocence. I was in that bed under the bright light and my forehead was against his. My arms were around him. We were together despite the plummeting gulf between my warm forehead and his cold forehead. The intimacies of years had made his forehead known to me, so well known that with his eyes shut and my eyes blinded, we were not lost to each other. Our knees together. My arm over his limbs. Everything that he was in that moment redeemed by love. *You did nothing wrong by not breathing for a long time*, I will think. *Your forehead is still known to me without seeing. I still feel it beneath my fingertip, no matter how cold it is.*

When he first assumed that position it was to sleep, not to die, and not to embrace his mum. I do not come to terms with him not reading this book. I simply don't. I continue to embrace him even from a distance of nine months—is that what it is? The birth of his new body to me? This first new embrace. It happened today, in the car, flying over the West Gate Bridge.

My other son missed his turn, and suddenly we were funnelled into the bridge, three lanes closed, *Summer Roadworks 26th Dec to 4th Jan* the sign was flashing. I remembered last year, when I said to you, 'Summer roadworks! They announce it like it's some kind of festival. Summer roadworks in Melbourne. Enjoy the holiday season.' We laughed with the adventure of life ahead of us; we were going to sit in Japanese cafés, walk up Turkish alleyways, comment together on being in a plane and look down at the clouds (a view you never saw except from heaven but you have seen more of their undersides than most, always looking to the sky that last summer, always expecting …)—we were off together on our lives at last, and I could see your sneakers on the dashboard of the van, your legs, your presence there … and that other one, my old self, not realising that I was in possession of all the world's rainbows and unicorns, gold coins raining on my head as in the fable, flowers and fruits springing up wherever my gaze strayed. I had no idea.

This time, today, with my other son, something returned to me.

It would take over an hour just to cross the bridge and return over it. The traffic was barely moving. I looked down and saw a boat, so distant, and thought of the bridge too thick with motionless cars and giant trucks and my heart fluttered, in the hope of fleeing the collapse. The bridge might collapse under all this weight. Had I ever before been a passenger on this bridge? This must be what you saw when I drove you over the West Gate, this must be how you felt looking down at the tiny boats.

Now, after nine months of you lying in your cave, the summer solstice passed, the comfort of the Christmas dream still with me, my son wound my window down automatically in the middle of the traffic jam on the West Gate. I thought there might be a headwind, my son inexplicably said. Meanwhile, a sudden wind, as beautifully cool as a drink of spring water, intensely sweet and strong, blew upon me steadily and I closed my eyes.

I love it, I said. *I feel like I'm on a boat*. This is how you speak to the living.

The other conversation is different and it goes on underneath and over the top.

So the fear of death went away, I opened my heart to it. Baby steps. After nine months, like your infant, I wriggle close to your still chest, I put my warm arm over you, lie there with you, neither of us moving, just glad to be together.

For a while now I've been afraid of the word 'still'.

I try to say it now.

I still love you. What is still still moves me, like the biggest wave, it doesn't ever stop.

I am afraid of what does not move. No. I am not afraid of what doesn't move but of that which, by your not moving, has been set in motion.

34

A Dirty Piece of Paper

SISTER WOULD you be able to—

Yeah of course sister come with me to the ATM I thought you were stressed—

It's just I have five kids and—

Don't worry about it, just come with me to the ATM and I'll get some money out, I don't carry cash I thought you looked stressed hello baby hello darling—

Thanks I just don't like to ask people—

Don't worry about it I had a lot of years with my three, ten dollars, five dollars, seven dollars, two dollars, a hundred dollars, ten dollars, two dollars—

That's how it is for me—

I know I know what it's like but the kids are the best part—

I had my first experience when I was eighteen—

Oh my mum was twenty when she had me—

Smart woman—

Oh you think she was old!—

I had my first at eighteen and now I have five—

That's the best I wish I had more—

For real?—

They are the best everything else is nothing I lost my son this year I don't know why now I'm broken you know what I mean I don't care I'm done you know—

Thank you—

Don't worry about it it's just money—

I just need it for food—

It doesn't matter what you need it for it doesn't matter just spend it on yourself anything at all it's just money do you know what I mean—

It's just a dirty piece of paper—

35

Out of Here

I BEGAN TO feel a certain fear. I realised that whether I allowed myself to be stabbed or run away, my end had come. Would it not be better, then, to run away and thus expose myself to a difficult and therefore more painful death? I could not immediately put my finger on the reasons in favour of this form of death, but I couldn't afford to spend my last remaining seconds looking for reasons.

I wonder now what passage it was in my father's worn-out copy of Kafka's stories that made you look up and say to me, 'I've never related to a writer like this before.'

I can guess.

It may have been:

I realised it was much later than I had thought and that I had to hurry; the shock of this discovery made me feel uncertain of the way, I wasn't very well acquainted with the town as yet; fortunately, there was a policeman at hand, I ran to him and breathlessly asked him the way. He smiled and said: 'Are you asking me the way?'

> *'Yes,' I said, 'since I can't find it myself.' 'Give it up! Give it up,' said he, and turned with a sudden jerk, like someone who wants to be alone with his laughter.*

You mentioned that line.

Or was it that so-called aphorism?

> *There is a hole in the back of his head so that all the world sees in. The one thing that upsets him is that he himself is denied this view.*

It was probably a combination. Of course it was. And yet, I believe that the moment you looked up from the book, you had just finished the famous last lines of 'The Departure'.

> *… 'Where is the master going?' 'I don't know,' I said, 'just out of here, just out of here. Out of here, nothing else, it's the only way I can reach my goal.' 'So you know your goal?' he asked. 'Yes,' I replied, 'I've just told you. Out of here—that's my goal.'*

Was it innate, or did you catch it from me—the desire for escape? Stronger than any desire I've ever known. When you went, it went for me.

I don't feel it anymore. The desire for escape, it turns out, is what others call hope.

I remember again those last conversations. 'I can't see myself having any kind of future here.'

You tired of the city long before I did for the simple reason that you knew more of it. You were the one who was punched in the face for wearing pink, you were the one who felt a knifepoint at your stomach at the train station. It was you who spoke semi-fluently the language of the otherworldly young man you often saw there, and who, you told me, knows everything and is exactly as he should be. It was you who walked hours and hours, four hours at a time, six hours at a time, from evening to sunrise, going only God knew where, at a tender age, until your shoes wore through completely. I still have those shoes here and I can prove how far you've walked. My shoes do not tell that story.

Ah, I remember your father's need for incessant movement now. And with him it manifested in a sometimes cruel utopian vision. Is my utopian vision cruel? Was yours? No. I don't believe you saw any such place. You saw it like Kafka.

When you said no future here, it might as well have meant 'in the world' because you couldn't remember any other world and had not seen much of it. We never had the money for camping or holidays. Moving states three or four times, from community and expulsion in the suburbs of the south, to temperate rainforest and expulsion from the south-south-east, then north on the ferry and bypassing those scenes that would be later and those places you would walk, and further north into the rural zones. The happy day we arrived in the rural town to Frosty Flakes and fresh milk in a fridge I didn't have to find or beg for. A furnished house. What a relief. A university house. And then onward to expulsion and the continuing desperate ploy to find a suitable school for you.

It is not an accident that so many Australian films are violent and oppressive.

Then we called it 'going through the tunnel' or 'the day you went through the three-hour tunnel'. To be fourteen, from a rural school, never having done more than an hour's worth of homework in your life due to conditions beyond your control, and then to sit a three-hour exam in the Royal Exhibition building …

When we saw all those youths, a sea of students in which we were swimming, trying to find the entrance, trying to figure out what was going on (what was going on?), I realised you were a minority in more ways than one. Many of them looked neat and studious too. We were pretty much a straight-D family, although I had found that the ingrained habit of desperate problem-solving worked for university assignments. Maybe it lent a certain intensity. The difference between high school and an arts course (yes, an arts course) was that, for the latter, Poverty and Resourcefulness marry well. Yet, always and everywhere, the resources we needed were not the ones we could lay hold of. No one was teaching us to fish anytime soon. Maybe you would be alright? Maybe you would be able to? Maybe you would be safe and not slammed into lockers and abused anymore.

You went in. I don't remember what I did meanwhile. It's a blank. I found you easily again when you came out—one out of a thousand.

Months later, I got the email and didn't even know what it would mean to us. I remember coming out and standing by the stove, maybe you were cooking something.

'You got in.'

You were incredulous. Amazed.

Your results were off the charts. A person who had never had a moment of mental space to study or even think. You gave the lie to the whole system and no one appreciated that.

But you cared: you had somehow clung to poems and read them over and over as a child. You had borrowed the graphic-novel Bible from the library and read the whole thing. You cared a lot.

Later, we saw the offensive doctor who I hoped would help with your depression, and who had become immortalised in our family history by his famously unhelpful line, 'Who told you to feel bad? Why should you feel bad?'

He wasn't the only doctor, on hearing what school you weren't attending enough, who said some version of 'Are you kidding me? I've been training my kids since prep to get into that school, hours of homework a night, and you are throwing it away?' And, he repeated, 'Why should you feel bad anyway? What do you feel so bad about?'

But I never expected that the school would bring you even deeper alienation and violence. I didn't understand that anyone would lay on the shoulders of one exhausted boy thousands of years of social conflict and history and expect you, or anyone, to be able to carry it. It was naive of me not to see you as representative of something, or to see that others would see you that way. Later you would say that you are responsible for the deeds of your ancestors and I would gasp and say No. No! That can't be right! But now I know why you felt that way. To me your struggle was real. It is real.

Feeling bad didn't cut any mustard. Depression and abuse. Depression because of abuse. Abuse because of depression. A young man. No father. No extended family. No community or social support. In the houses I rented and couldn't afford, we were always a room short. I was getting high grades in philosophy exams but I didn't know how to fill out the form for social or government housing. I kept getting partway through it. In that house, the house that went with the application to that school, I had given you the incongruous choice of your own room while my sixteen-year-old and eight-year-old shared a room with a cupboard in between them. At that time, you could barely see, barely know, barely walk.

And yet you'd passed the test. Your English was off the charts. Your maths surprisingly high as well, a situation I would never have found myself in, not ever.

You barely spoke. I wrote upside down and backwards for years and still can. I see numbers any old which way and often can't remember them. You were colour blind. I never found out if you could write well but later you came to speak with great directness and alacrity.

'For the first time in my life, this is a school I can be proud to go to because I earnt it.'

Not so much. Pride gave way to shame so soon. Years later you told me that every night you cried yourself to sleep.

The personal timing was good but the social timing was terrible: you had fled into an environment when certain wagons were pulling into a cynical circle. For so many reasons, we couldn't find a safe place to stand.

The few times I was there, I overheard other parents talking about their awful tenants and their renovations. They had trained their kids for years to get into the select-entry school so that they could save money on private school fees and avoid joining the rabble. Two for one deal.

Our life was different. There were times when your mum saw genuine caloric benefit in the stale bread on the car floor after dropping you off to school, bread that had fallen out of your school bag a few days before. A bird would have done the same, it's only natural. Matthew 6:26. But I did feel a bit sick when I found myself admiring a man's change shelf in his car's console while he was in the petrol station and I was in the passenger seat, on the way to an outing together. It was a glittering treasury in there full of gold pieces, more than I had in the bank. Our struggles were real. They are real.

Your physical symptoms were real too. The doctors did not believe in them. We were so tolerant while they smiled and failed us, or sneered and failed us, or didn't even look up and failed us, over and over. I am quite sure you would forgive them but I struggle to. Your pain and fatigue was, for them, either anxiety or the tall tales of a school refuser. (Later, I would read what they hadn't read, I would talk to cardiologists they did not refer you to: 'Heart pain can often be mistaken by children for stomach pain or back pain'; 'a young person could think their chest pain is anxiety'—especially if a doctor tells them so without checking.) They chastised us. I should know better. My son should be a man.

That wasn't easy either, was it? How could it be easy? I still have friends who are fifty but who think it's fine to say,

'Men are the only thing wrong with this world. Do they really think they can say anything worth hearing? Do they really think they have any problems?'

I had to take you out of school due to fear of your falling in front of the train. Not all of the kids there were cruel. Some of them were your good friends. Someone had pulled you back. You were dismissed by doctor after doctor. You were fifteen.

Some of the staff at that school were very kind to us. Your humanities teacher said to me: 'That child is absolutely incredible, I'm telling you. I've taught for decades. A student like this doesn't come around often, it's a unicorn. This is a very special young man. He can do anything, university lecturer, whatever, anything at all. I can't wait to find out what he's going to do.'

He remained one of the few male heroes you had. How many were there in the end? The father, son, and holy ghost? No, you weren't a trinitarian. (I want to ask you about that.) Other than Jesus, there was him—the humanities teacher—and your pastor at the end. That was all after a string of false leads and toxic influencers, I guess. I still think now and then that I should tell your humanities teacher what you ended up doing. And the unbearable final address.

'I just don't see any future for myself in Melbourne,' you said.

You loved that teacher the way water loves the touch of a human fingertip, the way that it just wants to be known.

If you're reading this, he sends you his thanks.

And then there was that day—were you already sick? What was it? (The hospitals wouldn't let us both in at once—it was that time. I was too scared to leave you in the care of strangers without a translator.) Your six-foot lanky body cuddled up to me like a grown-up joey trying to get back to mother's pouch and you said to me, forehead crinkled and desperation in your eyes, 'Promise me you'll get me out of here.'

The years of struggle were funnelling to an unbearable point. It wasn't just you. It was real. It wasn't what they call in school 'a lack of resilience'—that ship, if it ever existed, had sailed before you were born. It was suffering. It was the real fear of real conditions.

Yes. I will.

Promise me.

I promise.

Like Hamlet you said it in high distress, running out of the tunnel towards the light, *Swear!*

But you were gone before I could achieve it. All I can say to you, or could or would say to you is, don't forget that I bought three cat carriers for the plane. That proves I was serious. We were going to get out of here together. We were going to get out. I was going to fix everything.

36

Recover What?

37

YODO

IT DOESN'T seem like long ago that the kids, not just mine, but the kids in general, were saying YOLO and being silly like that. I enjoyed their implicit critique of reincarnation, for only the Resurrection interests me. And yet, I also like, 'Before Adam, there were a thousand Adams.'

Yet I have felt my beloved son die so many deaths over the last nine months. There have just been so many, so many. I felt it so many times in my heart when you were here, and I feel it still—the variation, the repetition, the replay of deaths, as if there were an inexhaustible quantity of angles from which to see the saddest thing, the most sacred thing, that I have ever known. It becomes a Kaaba.

What a privilege it is, and was, to be alone.

For you too?

I saw in your notebook, *I have almost died so many times*.

You were right. I felt it too. Why didn't we talk about it? Is it for the same reason as these people now do not talk about it with me?

All these that could happen, all those that might have happened, converge into that one place and time. Necessity demands that the number be reduced to one or even none.

'Do not think of those who died fighting in God's cause as dead, for they are ever living.'

You might be surprised at the causes listed for qualification to the status of martyrdom, other than righteous warfare (if that exists): they include dying by drowning, or in an epidemic or a pandemic, or by a blow, including a car accident, or of a stomach sickness—and stomach, I have read, means any part of the body.

And that is as much as I am willing to think about it for tonight.

38

Death

IS IT to be this one then? This? When I nearly lost you so many times?

I remember the time I lay in my bed, in my thirties and in university housing,* and it was pouring rain like it is now. After a decade of drought, a rainstorm. Tremendous rainstorms come after heat and drought. I was in bed reading *The Tempest* and only years later did I make the connection.

It has been so hot here since New Year's Eve that I can barely cope. I can't work, I can't write, I can't think. I've put on maybe twenty kilos since the lightning bolt hit me, as if I'm trying to sink into the ground with you, or as if my metabolism no longer works, or as if I no longer know who I am as an individual, so I'm finally free to surrender to all that genetic weight brought to bear since Nan's husband arrived in this

* Once, University Services came in while we were out, without word or warning, invading what we were all naively imagining as our family home, and an unknown person chopped our op shop toaster's cord in two. I didn't know what 'tagging and testing' was and only understood later.

country (and who knows what before that). We suffer here as though generations of malnutrition, addiction, anxiety, workaholism and depression are magnetically pulling us into miserable lives and early graves. You had it from both sides of your family. Did I inherit poor choices from my mother, my grandmother too? How to know a good man when you don't know a good man? Well, I knew one, and it was you, I gave birth to two (opinion verified by external sources).

So it was a rainstorm, like now, and I was in bed by my window, which faced the road, reading *The Tempest*. Sometimes, I was still young enough that I'd run outside when it rained, with or without you kids, and delight in getting drenched, as if I was thirsty for that mercy, and I was. I even lay in it by the roadside as it gushed down from the slick over-mined slopes of the sparse gum forest. The muddy torrent was delicious to me. My whole body craved it, I don't know why. I took a dip in it. Ten years' drought.

Back then the university was surrounded by bush, and my house was one of the last before the hill and the water catchment drains. On the other side of the road, a little rocky gully, always dry, led us up to the oval (which is now a carpark, the machines came and continued until we left. It made me sick in my stomach, the cat too—she walked with her belly close to the ground, tail down, all the time intimidated by the low rumble)—and that gully, of who knows what? Old barbed wire embedded in clay as hard as rock, large sharp rocks embedded there, dirt slopes. It's where we crossed, across the small cul-de-sac, gravel edged, walking between the trees, down into that hard clay gully, and up, towards the childcare centre and the university. This was also where the kangaroos crossed from the sports field, through the gully to come to our house. Their families would come into our yard every day to graze.

In bed, during the tempest, I suddenly realised I couldn't hear you, none of you—of course not—the rain—and that I didn't know where you were. A sudden flash inside me like the flash flood, of fear—I wasn't sure of what. (Death.)

The weather was suddenly less exultant and only menacing.

The baby was fine.

I ran out into the downpour. Your brother I found poking around somewhere in that bush across the road. Always a careful sort. But you—nowhere to be seen and my eyes flew to the voluminous gushing torrent that used to be our little dry gully. Where we always went and you often played.

'Where—?' I yelled. Your brother shrugged.

'Go inside and stay with your sister!'

I screamed your name, again and again, and looked with hollow eyes down at that swelling brown torrent that broke over all submerged rocks and wire, now carrying branches in full flight, and everything it could sweep from the slick and steep mud sides, fully cleared of debris and too dangerous to approach even for me. Slick slides. You must have been nine. I can't do the maths. Who cares? My little boy.

I backed away from those mudslide edges, one step there would be the end. I saw it all. The head hit on the rocks, the twisted body submerged showing up later in the day somewhere when the water subsided, somewhere at the end of my street. Not far but out of my grasp forever. Then I saw you, right at the edge, on that so-slippery ground, swinging yourself over the torrent, holding a young tree with one hand, poking at the surface of the water with a stick.

'Don't move!' I cried. You smiled, happy to see me, happy playing there.

It wasn't the end. I took you inside. You must have thought I was crazy. Worrying about a little bit of rain and a nice, surprising stream. There weren't that many nice surprises.

So is this it, then? This one? We have to settle for it? We can't keep imagining the others anymore? Will there be no more work to do for that muscle inside me that knows exactly how to fear your death? Yours and not any other, specific to you?

I know, so well, how to fear it. What I do not know is how to accept it. I cannot believe this is not just one in the many I imagined. Admittedly, this one that you and God arranged privately, without my involvement, is probably the best. I don't think I had a better one. Even entering your flat, when I rushed in the dark to the bathroom, that fleeting imaginary one was a worse one than the one I then found, which has no name but only the bare fact. It is unascertained. Officially.

Cause: unascertained.[*]

In my heart, and to your church, you are akin to Enoch. You outlived so very much but then you were gone, for God took you.[**]

* They told me it would be a lot of trouble to change the certificate but I'm working on it.

** Genesis 5:24. And Enoch walked with God and then was seen no more, for God took him.

And now the rain outside recedes from this different road (a road on which you've never lived or perhaps ever walked down—I'll never know), the debris piled up in the middle of the road as the flooding slips back towards the gutters. The event is past. This is the theory about it: the event is past.

Theory.

Theories of time, theories of people.

This is not a grief memoir. It can be a love story, such as people don't write enough because parents and childhoods are pathologised, and because mothers are women and because sex sells.

The relief I felt when I found you swinging by one arm from the skinny tree, drooping over the deluge in the tempest, even while I imagined you losing your grip or slipping—it was immense. This relief is something I will never again feel in my body in this life.

It is beyond good. It is the feeling of being restored to yourself, being rebuilt suddenly, miraculously. It is like a resurrection. You must have felt saved like that yourself.

For me, it was always you that held me over the edge and saved me. I don't begrudge you that. I take it naturally, as if it is your right. It is your right.

Death, to the living (if I imagine being a materialist), is just a little stop. It is just a breath not taken, a heartbeat not performed, and a circulation not carried out. It is not anything. It is that you used to breathe and then, at a certain time, you didn't breathe, that's all. It is as if something carried on for a while, like a piece of music, an activity, a beehive on an old porch somewhere, and then it stopped happening. Something stopped, but life flows on.

For me (not a materialist and permanently immersed in the highest and most profound love I know), what stopped has caused all of life to swell around it. This stop in the river of life, this abyss where before was something consistent—you—causes such a change in the flow of things that it is as if a waterfall now plummets where before we just stood by the little stream and led our lives. This stop, this little gap in your breathing habits has made everything new. When I hold my breath, or breathe out and don't allow myself to inhale, something starts to balloon out in my chest, something starts to rush—it must be the start of this waterfall you created—it reminds me now of how, when Nan breathed out her last breath, the birds outside her window, quiet all day, erupted in a cacophony.

So here I am with this gigantic, amazing waterfall in front of me. Now I can't go out. There is no ford, no crossing, as long as I remain here. Everything is different.* New trees and animals will come. The sound, I may get used to it, or I may always struggle to hear what is going on around me. And in this beautiful mist I hope I will eventually see our rainbow appearing. I am looking for it, that's all I'm looking for.

* 1 Corinthians 15:51–52. Behold, I shew you a mystery; we shall not all sleep, but we shall all be changed, in a moment, in the twinkling of an eye, at the last trumpet: for the trumpet shall sound, and the dead shall be raised incorruptible, and we shall be changed.

39

My Phone Is Dead

SILENCE HAS almost arrived.

It has happened the way suffocation scenes happen in films or in dreams.

It has been agonisingly hard to silence this phone. It's still not over but it's gone too far to stop now and the silence is inevitable. The constant buzzing and ringing of years ago is well and truly over. The rhythms of requests and arrangements, the back and forth. It dwindled. Its silence started to be loud. I don't like it when people use that phrase my phone is dying, my phone is dead. Not just because of trauma, although it hasn't helped. I don't actually say the d-word out loud myself. A game offered to my children that horrified me: look after a virtual pet. Feed it, water it, play with it. If you forget—as you would since it's not a living being—it sickens and dies and it's your fault.

If it's going to buzz and ring again soon, it's not dead.

Some people are nurturing relationships with their phones like with newborns, but even more intensively. They have even made it an impossible thing to say, it clichéd itself so fast no one had time to think about it. You can't criticise phones, rectangles of doom. You just have to keep going, responding and responding and responding. Now if it stirs I pick it up and silence it swiftly.

The phone is a virtual pet. There are no relationships to the living or dead inside of it. No one is waiting for us there. I guess no one ever was.

Days pass now and nothing. Sometimes weeks. It has been quite some time since I spoke to an adult I didn't give birth to. They're all gone, I have slipped out from between their rhythms of response and perhaps from their thoughts as well.

I don't say 'we' very often when it comes to this, but now I will: if it seems that sometimes we allow people to treat us badly, it is not because we are weak. We allow people to treat us badly because we see it as an extension of their nature and we are not in the business of changing people. We are not in the business of restricting people's freedom. And since it is not in our nature, we are not much affected by it either. We have a high tolerance. But then, we have a very low tolerance for the other kind of thing: if you do not respect us, we will find out and it will be over, not because we choose for it to be over but because it is already over. Others can make use of us. But if I am merely an entertainment or a resource, it will be over, because it's over. That will not be our choice. Not being part of our lives, you will not be part of our lives. You will return to where you already are—far from us. If we are alone, we are alone.

Like Kafka, who said this about marriage, *I admire relationships in general, and in their infinite variety; I do not admire any particular relationship; the happiness of any particular relationship, even in the best case, would crush me with despair*. I did try to have fun for a short while, which I bitterly regret. It took me away from the one who was central and for whom I should have been preparing food.

In the last analysis, it was an entertainment device. Like all entertainment, it is enervating and manipulative. It played me.

Now it's me and the window again.

40

Waiting for the Invisible Signal

TODAY I stood with my hand under the running tap. It has been so hot lately that the water out of the cold tap felt warm. I waited and I waited.

I used to be so worried about wasting anything but you were right, sometimes you need to think about yourself and your own comfort too. You vindicated me. I felt you standing there, with your finger under the tap, unashamed to run the water until it turned cold, waiting for the invisible signal.

We never trusted the pipes of any of our rental houses. Once, the water ran clear, but it was unbelievably bitter. I spat out my mouthful of it and searched the internet about the taste, seeking information about possible poisons (it was copper). Who knew what condition the pipes were in?

Wasn't it always that way with me, worrying about lead in the flaking paint of your windowsills, about the fibres of deteriorated carpet floating in sunbeams, about the creeping damp?

Your allergies were always so bad, you said it was like knives in your eyes. The cats didn't seem to be the cause. And then there was the occasional news report of someone's children dying due to carbon monoxide from the gas heater. I spun the wheel and gambled: if we moved enough times we could escape accumulated poisons. A bit of lead from one windowsill would be cancelled out by a bit of DDT from another yard, which would be cancelled out by the occasional fumes or asbestos or funny-tasting water.

I held my hand under the tap for a long time today, waiting for the water to tell me it was free of this random house and its invisible circumstances, and that I'd be in contact with the more general source, the more egalitarian pipelines, not just these contingent, risky, personal pipes that fate had put me in line with.

I still worry: was it the mouse shit I found in the drawers of your flat? The peppermint oil you had used to combat them? Damp? Mould? A certain food? A supplement? A neighbour? A relative? Trauma? The past? My second of hesitation on the phone when you said you thought you should move back in with me and I worried about you losing your first and only chance at the private rental game? 'Don't lose your rental reference, it's so hard to get that.' Was that what did it? Broken heart? It's enough to almost kill me now but I'm trying. I'm trying and I'm waiting to get in touch with something beyond all this.

The water never runs cold, not really. It tastes sour.

I regret not arriving at your house one day with an air purifier and a hundred litres of spring water. Plastics? BPA? You didn't have a car, so it must have been the hardest thing for you to shop for. Especially if something was weakening you inside. (Was it?*) I remember how I used your spring water cask as a footrest at that bus stop, the last time we were together. But I never thought of delivering some to you. Some stupid dream about independence, that you or I or both of us were having. Independence. A fool's dream.

I should have driven you up into the cool and leafy mountains where we could both drink from the spring that horses used to drink from.** It turned out it was only an hour away then, but now it's an eternity. If I find it, may you be there waiting for me, with a full cup.

---

* Yes.

** Mount Donna Buang. I went there, later, with my daughter, drank a lot and, as we drove away, I imagined I had probably been poisoned. How fast do springs flow? How long had that water been there? How diluted? Who trusts a public spring on a mountain full of acid-addled boomers these days?

41

The Heat

DOESN'T IT seem selfish to complain about the senses—about having them at all? About the feeling body—having life? Doesn't it seem selfish when someone else, just nineteen, would have turned twenty and didn't? Whose body no longer works and whose senses are not feeling the cold damp ground. Even so, my dear son, I find a way to complain about the heat. You know what I'm like. Even sitting there at your grave a few days ago, stroking the slender tufted stems of vanilla grass that sway in the air so gently by your wooden post, I say *it's hot today*. I always wait until near sunset because I can't sit there any earlier under the sun, but then I get stressed about closing time. You know what I'm like. I get all this stress bottled up inside me, stress from way back, stress from all the times I nearly lost it, and nearly lost you, and still can nearly not cope at all.

At home, during these heat waves, I imagine myself making a short film as a fat and sweaty single mum. The film has two parts. 'How I spent the summer' and 'How my landlords spent the summer'. It's a bit clichéd, to be honest.

I'm upstairs, clambering onto a bedside table trying to hang the silver car windscreen sunshield in between the blinds and the window, which is that zone of high convection in the afternoons. I dream of coating the blind with cooking foil so that it goes up and down and I don't have to do this. In the morning the sun heats up your brother's room. It passes over the roof and when it touches my windowsill I know what is going to happen. There will be seven hours of relentless western sun turning my room into a sauna, quite literally. I am pouring with sweat wearing nothing but an old nightie because I can't wear clothes anymore in the house. I jump up on that table and try to hang the car windscreen shield in the window, blinded by the folds of foil. It falls down and I rehang it in a variety of ways every day. Tape melts. Pins fall out. The blind doesn't hold it. It crumples and I jump back up. It's the only exercise I can do.

Cut to my landlords. How are they spending the afternoon? I picture them feeling cool enough that they can even go outside to water the plants because they know they can come back into the air-conditioned lounge. Their laptop doesn't overheat. They can concentrate on TV. They can even cook food in their kitchen.

Cut to me again, standing in front of the freezer, fanning myself with the freezer door until I hear the warning beep, listening to the crackle of my food defrosting slightly.

Cut to my current landlord, who is cool enough.

Cut to me, sweating and holding my matted hair up with my hand because in my heat exhaustion I have lost the hair clips. I can't find anything. Everything is falling, especially the car windscreen shield makeshift blinds. I haven't experienced being cool enough for many days and nights in a row. I am hot and sweating every minute of the day and night. I go into the cold shower frequently. I forgot what feeling dry is like, I am semi-amphibian now. When the sun finally sets, my room remains sauna-like. No airflow. I stand by my window and pull down the half-collapsed car windscreen shield and the streetlight shines in. I put the blind half down and spend some time yanking it back and forth, trying to suck night air from the street into the house but it doesn't happen. I don't know why I cannot get air into this house.

Cut to my landlord. What is he doing? Does he even know our downstairs sink tap doesn't work and we have to wash our hands in the kitchen sink after using that toilet? Does that matter? Sure, you can wash your hands anywhere. I picture my landlord sitting on a leather couch, cool enough to do that. I picture my landlord able to do exercise, go shopping, walk in the street, read or work, do household chores or relax. Even drink a hot cup of coffee. All I can do is sweat and stress, listening to the sound of my heart squeaking in my ears, the sound of rushing in my head, putting on kilo after kilo of water weight, feeling migraines coming on, feeling nausea, joint pain, feeling unable to care for anyone, unable to feel the grief I need to feel, unable to cry for fear of headache, forgetting to put water out for birds, spending too much on takeaway, waiting, waiting for months to pass so I can feel dry and get dressed. Thinking, it's only another six weeks tops and I'll feel better.

I'll be teaching online again. That's a good thing. I'll be downstairs with a fan facing me and no one will know or care if I don't have shoes on. You would think I would prefer to work on campus in an air-conditioned room. Not so—I'm a casual. That would mean getting dressed in this sauna and going out into the street and getting to that room—something I cannot imagine facing without ten minutes of coolness first. There are not ten minutes of coolness in this house and February has just started. I can't imagine leaving the house under these circumstances and presenting myself in public.

Cut to my landlord, who enjoys $580 per week from me and my son (almost my whole PhD stipend, which I struggled for most of my kids' childhoods to achieve), while we enjoy his currently uninhabitable sickness-producing house. What is he doing? What is he counting off the weeks towards? A temperature drop or a holiday? Why hasn't he installed an air conditioner here so that it's liveable for those Melbourne months when we get heat waves?

And the worst thing is, I wonder how hard February was for you, the month before you went, my beloved one, because at that time, in the old house I got kicked out of, I had air conditioning and you didn't. We were separated for a time. How hot was it at your place? Is that why I didn't see you as much in the last two months of our time together on Earth? When you said you were going to spend some time alone, going to do a bit of reading? And did the heat contribute to your hardship? Did it contribute to your illness? (I cannot think the next thought.) Because your landlord didn't install an air-conditioning unit?

The anger phase is not happening today and it is not happening on any day. It is off limits. I am not someone who will be experiencing an anger phase. I only see it on the horizon occasionally and then I swim away into the other more comfortable zones. But I do see it sometimes when I try to come up for air and find none for my son. None for so many people. It's not charitable of me to be reverse-classist and bitter and imagine my landlord's life is perfect. It's a bit ugly to write about my problem with perspiration when so many people have to suffer so much worse than my own disability, my own illness- and class-based challenges, and I only want to bear witness to these things for my son's sake, for all my children's sakes. It's not nice to complain, not ever.

The last few nights I dreamt of dead bodies, of weeping intensely in grief with chest pain, of looking inside an empty coffin, of vomiting. Sometimes I just feel all this stress is bottled up inside me. The heat doesn't help.

Some rental advocacy organisation has been spamming me about improving housing conditions. They want me to be a volunteer by putting a thermometer in my house over either the summer or the winter.

42

Fearful Sleep

I AM STILL waking up every day thinking someone will be dead. It doesn't help that all of us sleep in to random hours, reminding me of all the stories:

I thought she was asleep. I left her till noon. Then I started to wonder if she was okay.

He usually sleeps in, so I wasn't worried until …

I went out and when I came back after work it was obvious that he hadn't been up. I got concerned, so …

I had the longest sleep I'd had since she was born and …

We are flatmates and I hadn't seen him around for a few days for some reason. He's awake all night, sometimes he's gaming and then he sleeps most of the day. My other flatmate hadn't seen him for a while either. We tried his phone and the battery was flat. Then …

I wondered why the cat was scratching at my housemate's door so much.

I heard our dog barking in the middle of the night at our son's room but by the time …

He wasn't up for school so I went to wake him and …

All horror stories that start with sleep.

With my son, I alternate between checking and waiting. It is a great blessing that he has a morning sneezing habit that I can hear from my room. I love it. But with my daughter, this summer holiday, she stays up with insomnia all night and sleeps all day. I check on her at odd hours with varying degrees of panic. I look for movement. Even the slightest movement is a sign of hope. There is almost nothing that will induce me to enter the room and touch her if I haven't seen that. Her doona is thick and bunchy. Sometimes it is hard to detect movement and I stand there squinting, looking for the movement of anything, even a hair, and glancing in horror towards her feet if they are out of the covers, as his were, and looking for medical facts I don't even know the name of but that I saw. Then I rush over and touch the doona sometimes.

She used to be a heavy, heavy sleeper. Now she wakes up at the sound of the door handle. She never remembers me. She doesn't know that some days I come in about six or seven times before she wakes up for real. We even converse. I put on a light tone and say 'Morning! How did you sleep?', etc. I don't know if she buys it.

43

125L of Earth

IT'S SUNDAY and 32 degrees Celsius with strong sun and high humidity. I do two kilometres on the Walking Pad and wait for the sun's painful progress over our house to reach my western windows. I put up the silver windscreen foils behind my blinds so it doesn't convect as much up there in my bedroom. My kids were a bit worried how that would look from the road. I wasn't, but when I checked all I noticed was that the neighbouring terrace has two air conditioners on their roof. It must be nice in there.

All day I was leaning into the last hours of light when I would go and add to the 'mother' soil at your resting place.* I only go in the last hour of light. Golden hour.

I told my son, I have two things I need help with. You will not want to do either of them but the first you will probably not mind too much.

---

* Some call the soil that is replaced into a grave following a burial 'the mother,' perhaps because it protects the vulnerable body there, which some mothers would do.

So we picked up the five bags of soil from the local IGA. Three bags of potting mix and two of garden soil, you helped me buy them and load them into the car and went into Woolworths for flowers and cold spring water for me to drink, and then I proceeded to the graveyard alone.

I used that suitcase we put my work computer into when we had to pack up my office at the start of the pandemic. I didn't want to touch the suitcase because of that, knowing the last time I used it, you were helping me carry something heavy, helping me carry it to our last home together, where I set up my little office in the lounge room alongside my bed, and where everything spiralled into chaos and …

But it was the only way to carry the soil, anyway.

It only took two trips from the car.

I thought that I would feel I was burdening you, tipping that big pile on top of where your stomach would be. But it felt fluffy and light, as I spread it out with my hands. I remembered, at that moment, that your brother had even hugged me when he gave me the flowers and the spring water. 'Don't breathe that soil in too much, it's toxic'—as if I care! But I love that he cared.

My heart felt so full to be there in the heat of early evening restoring your resting place to a good state. After the rainstorms, the concavity was deep. Last week, at first I had imagined the boards under there had caved in, had seen Poe-style horrors in my mind, but it was paranoia. It's just the soil compacting.

'Settling,' they call it.

They are hardy flowers, the white ones, on either side of your head. Even in these weeks of heat and blasting sun, and the infrequent watering and shallow soil from my last attempt to cover the clay, they are still holding on and putting out tiny little white stars. And the white heliotrope at the post, which I thought dead and gone and buried, has emerged from the ground, a little shoot from its former self. The vanilla grasses are thriving and have gone to seed with delicate, downy little tops. The yellow flowers needed deadheading and have plenty of buds.*

It's my only garden and the only bit of ground I own. If it was a bit bigger I could just live there under a bit of tin or something. Would there be any food? I would need food. Maybe if some of the other mothers came to live there too, on their tenures, we could find a way, between us, to live.

I dreamt of that. The graveyard was a place of archways and overhanging vines.

I felt like I was making a cake, spreading out the fluffy black soil. It was more like caring for you and tucking you in than it was like burying. Of course, I'm sorry about the Brunnings brand and the toxicity, I wanted it to be pure, just humus, but the fact is, my dear, I couldn't manage more than a trip to the local IGA and to buy whatever potting mix and garden soil they sold there.

---

* All of this is gone now. The vanilla grass never self-seeded. In place of it, cuttings of geraniums I picked from around the suburb, which I stuck into the soil, thrived and offered their red, indigo and pastel pink love heart petals. The pastor, who said, 'I'm sorry I haven't visited the grave. I haven't had much experience of that,' arrived one day and placed a cross of twigs. His son came with him another time and put another cross beside it.

I couldn't do what I tried to do all along, to do everything perfectly and purely. Even something as important as this, for it feels important.

I just had to make do.

And the flowers of course, I've worked in flower factories, and I know how it is. It was good that I could afford it, or I know I would have been digging some soil from roadsides or maybe national parks, I don't know. It would have been an ordeal.

I watered the plants with a jug by someone else's grave. I ask him not to mind and to forgive me for borrowing it the times I forget to bring a water bottle or can. I ask for reward for him, for his participation in the beauty and growth of the plants and the good that it does.

This was all really quite easy, apart from the heat, and then I sat in the cool and pulled the heads off the fresh flowers and arranged them in a half-circle around your little wooden post, that says, incongruously, impossibly, implacably, your name.

I wiped it clean with tears and dirty hands and rested with my back to your end-neighbour's comfortable and shading stone. I realised there is room for a planter in between your post and the back of his broad and cool stone. It blocks the setting sun's rays, which I used to like receiving, but then, the shade is so welcome in the summer. Months ago, his wife cried to me, *they got it wrong, it looks like a bedhead don't you think, it looks like a bedhead, it is not what I asked, not what my son did, the drawings, he is an architect, you know* (or was it an engineer?). Anyway, they changed it for her because now the arches are higher and it looks like what she wanted. Though not a double bedhead, it's a double—she's waiting to join him at his left. (And there's an optional one on the side for her son, with fake grass and a bench, so as not to seem anticipatory, she said.) She was asleep next to him when she woke up to find she was the only one able to wake up. If only I had been asleep next to you like that, so I could have been there in the night in case, unbearably, you had needed me and had been unable to call for help, instead of where you were: alone with the Alone.

In the final rays of the day, after I'd talked to you for half an hour or so, a woman walked between the monuments carrying flowers in a bucket, sunburnt on her shoulders.

There's been an empire growing to the south of you. Broad and high, its beams and pillars have been growing over the months, sometimes shrouded in flapping plastic, loud in the wind. Now it's unveiled, with a huge photo of a chubby and grinning face gazing into the setting sun.

I don't know it yet but talking with this woman, or even just the hope of seeing her, will become a Sunday routine. It will bring unexpected warmth and comfort. One time she will light a candle for my son because I forgot my lighter. On another Sunday, she will lend me permanent access to her watering can in the special waterproof trunk she has had installed.

She turns to me and she looks just like him. She asks me the taboo and dreaded graveyard question, 'Who is it?' and 'How did it happen?'

But I don't mind with her and, besides, I'm lonely enough.

'My son too,' she says. 'I took him to hospital one day and he never came home.'

We try in vain to describe. We keep putting our hand over our chests. She weeps. We hug. Due to, I believe, not feeling safe as child, I don't cry around people; the reflex turns off in the company of others. ('People like that are a bit messed up,' my daughter said sympathetically, and it's true.) I do not want to call attention to myself.

'My son,' she says. 'He was my life.'

'You look just like him.'

'Everyone says that.'

'This is beautiful!' I tell her, throwing my arms out towards the structure, from where we are standing in the short distance between our sons' graves—though honestly my mind can hardly take it in. Apart from its large etching of her son gleaming in the last rays, with its expansive engraved back wall flanked by white pillars rising to an open ceiling, it neither resembles a tomb nor a building, but something that there may only be one of.

'I designed it. Some people say things … but you know … he would have loved it!'

'People shouldn't say things. It's beautiful.'

'It's his only home now for …'

'Eternity,' I fill in for her.

'Yes. Why do the good ones get taken?'

'I don't know …'

I drift back to you. Before I leave, she drifts over.

'You have real plants,' she says in admiration of our rectangle of soil.

'Only ever real plants,' I say.

She lowers her voice so as not to offend anyone, 'I don't believe in fake flowers.'

'Me either,' I whisper.

The graveyard closed forty-five minutes ago. We are the only two there.

'It feels different, better, when there are fresh flowers and plants.'

'I believe that fresh flowers or leaves remember God on their behalf, because they are living.'

I kiss my fingertips and touch the dirt.

44

The Bonds of Life*

MY HEART is broken. There is an elephant sitting on my chest. All of the fun has gone out of life. I feel like I weigh a tonne. I don't want to be here anymore. I want to sink into the earth. I don't exist anymore but I have to get up every day. I breathe with a small shallow place at the bottom of my chest. I breathe in the bottom of my breath in small slow sections that make me exhausted. I forget that I can breathe in all the way and let my chest rise. It feels like exercise to do that. This is what they mean when they say *there is an elephant sitting on my chest.*

I visit the resting place, waiting for my friend to appear in the last rays of the sun, dragging the green bin across to her son's well-tended shrine. I associate suns and sons with her, and the last of the light. But she doesn't come. Her son's plants are drying and dying and I feel a growing sense of dread. When a man appears one day, I go over and ask him,

---

* On Kafka's gravestone is engraved, in Hebrew, *May his soul be bound in the bonds of Life.*

'Where is she?' He points to the ground, gestures to the new grave across from my son's, the new grave covered in fine white sand that I have been wondering about and even a little jealous of. Now I visit her, who was my Sunday sunset companion, as well as my son, and I miss her viscerally.

Everything is ruined. There is nothing in the world that I want to do or see and no one I want to be. There is nothing I want to do but I have to do it all anyway. I drag myself around. I drag what's left of myself around.

At the same time, I'm frightened. Very frightened of something that happened ten months ago. That happened last minute. That is about to happen. That will happen eternally. That may happen again to someone else that I love. The world is not a safe place. It never was and never will be.

I cannot reach anyone and no one can reach me. There is a space around me that I cannot fill. I talk to my son. He doesn't answer.

I talk to my son. I hear memories of his chuckle and his comment.

Visions float around in front of me, more real to me than what I'm looking at. I see his sneakers up on the dashboard even though I'm not in my car. I see the hair on his legs in the sun. I see his limbs, his elbow from the back under the sleeve of his T-shirt. When he was fifteen, sometimes his elbows were dirty from school desks. I see his shorts. I see his feet in those old worn-out sneakers that had walked around the world all over Melbourne. (Now in my stairwell.)

I see me and him in his house, me standing near the front door, my bag still over my shoulder, playing with his newly purchased bright red cordless vacuum cleaner, giving it a whirl and admiring it, him chuckling with self-conscious pride. You're ahead of the game here, I said, far out! And him saying I know, I know, but it's not quite as good as yours. I see his beautiful new bike that he bought online, bright orange to me—I never asked what colour it was to him. My memory is bad. I hear myself say, 'Oh! such a—!' I almost hear him say indistinct things. I can't see where he is standing or sitting but I feel his hesitancy and I feel that stupid dumb distance that exists between living people who share a world and love each other but are held back by the devil from expressing it freely. He did. He expressed himself more freely. He was more free. I remember his text message in the night that I didn't answer because I wanted to hold its reassurance with me as a gift and a treasure, to let him have the last word for once, *Good night ma. All the love* ♥ And how it was so so hard in the land of the living to tell someone how we feel but he often managed it. I stretch and reach as hard as I can for his voice, the best sound I have ever heard, but I can't quite catch it. There are no recordings.

Or maybe on that phone.

There will never be anger. Or else there will never be anything but anger and I'm inside the world of anger and I don't even know it. No. It's not the case. I know too much to be angry. And I have no anchor in its world. I know, for one thing, the faults and failings and the causes of the damage done to and by those who were supposed to be looking out for him. I know just by looking at them or not looking at them, or just listening to the silence of our phones over the years. I know they will persist in their being and their being silent like a stone subsists in being a stone. How to be angry at rocks? At fools? I can't do it. I see and I know what they did and didn't do, and I know their names, and I know their excuses, just as well as I know my own. Let them bury their dead. They have no place in this story. They can tell their own stories if they have the wit.

The relationship will never end. *They are ever living.* I do not say the d-word. I can write it but I will not say it. I may never say that phrase out loud. No thanks. And the relationship will never end. Shall I 'let go' of my own soul? Shall I 'move on' from my own heart? People who imagine this separation as a wound have never considered that there is no self left to wound. That's how it is for me. This is why I understand the 'terrible prayer', the prayer of a philosopher who didn't lose a child. The self that was wounded was mortally wounded. I died at forty-six, just like David Foster Wallace, only instead of my beloved finding me, I found my beloved son and my life was concluded in that moment.

Do you think it was different from that? Do you have neat and tidy ideas about who lives, who dies, who kills and is killed? Do you think I didn't plunge into the abyss and am now keeping house there? Let me tell you, apart from not having him here with me, this new life is better in every way than the illusion that preceded it, than the petty life of all that non-death, and, as for that rectangle of earth, I prefer it to the world and everything in it—except for my other children who are each as worthy of all this as he is, and a couple of people and ideas that I happen to like.

On a grief forum, someone says something like this and it upsets another.

Are you saying that if I don't have any surviving children my life is not worth living?

No, of course not!

But you did, you said, I keep going for the sake of my other children. That's what that means.

No, no, of course not, I only meant—

I don't say it, but I think it: those without surviving children, childless parents, do not wake up every day wondering if the axe will split them in half again the way I do. Some have already had it happen again. There is another world, a world of traumatic loss, that is further away than the furthest point on the earth from where some stand. There is no bridge. You cannot visit—perhaps that is why you don't. But let me assure you, if it wasn't for not having him with me, everything else about this is better. It's not that I'm better off—of course not. Only that life flows in to fill the space where I used to be. The suffering, the sickness, the struggle, the clinging to the edge, the shaking in the core, the fear—all of it is a gift of love. All because that's what life is. It's what life has always been. My reality. Not your yoga and your wellness and your income, your chakras, your beers, your drugs, your fantasies, your culture and class. The empty place I grew into as a child, as my self drained away, has been regained in fullness through love of my child. This love is eternal.

What a mighty metaphor God chose for the ultimate sacrifice: the loss of a child. God made my son so sweet that my eyes water until I'm dissolved. Who produced this sweetness?

This wonder? That's the only interesting question. Fools can keep the rest.

There is a ruby that contains the sunrise and afterwards the whole apparent world and the bridge to the next.

What I am saying is that I have too many rubies now. I am giving them away not because I'm generous but because they're heavy.

His bike is out there, I can see it through the bars of the window. I don't know quite how to get it fixed either and I don't want some weird inner-city cycling guy to touch it, not realising it is sacred. Just the other day, I saw the cause of the puncture in his back tyre. A screw. I imagine that silver screw, sitting upright in the road, and him (I never saw him on the bike, but I know: ordinary clothes, his shorts and hoodie, his sneakers, no helmet), riding towards it, looking to the horizon, on his last ride. It missed the front wheel but pierced the midline of the back tyre and went all the way in. He wouldn't have known it at first.

But then riding became hard. Then life became harder. He didn't call me. He must have walked the bike home and put it in his house, wondering what to do. By then he was used to hardship, waiting, aporia, chest pain, suffering, solitude. No car, no money, no way to fix it.

I think it was during our last phone call he told me that there was a Collective that might interest me, a place where I might be able to get a cheap and good bike (years ago, he had left mine unsecured at a train station, in a hurry to get to his break-up session of the 'in2school' program, and I had cried and cried like a fool, the last straw, I can't keep anything for myself, do I have to lock my things up at my own house? I can't trust even my own family to respect, blah blah blah), and people volunteer there to fix up old bikes, he said. It might help you, he said. He never mentioned the puncture. I see it there now.

Who left that screw in the road?

Who did this to us?

He never rode the bike again.

It meant he could walk to church in a suit the Sunday just before he left the world, before he returned home alone, took off his shirt, and his pants, and placed his dress shoes down by the bed and climbed into it. I believe he was very, very tired.

45

Afterword

Problem—
  my dearest beloved has turned away
facing the wall
  took off his dress shoes
laid himself out
  in bed
his last gestures.
  Solution?
God's promise is true
  There is an afterlife
There is beatitude
  and all our lives are soon coming to an end
and we mustn't worry about it—

Problem—
  he will not lie in the hammock with me
he will not sit on the couch with me
  he will not be in the car beside me
walk with me
  talk to me

I may forget his voice
  my most valued possession
the shape of his toes
  His hands
His face
  His ear I already cannot recall
or call back
  at all—

Problem—
  My beloved has gone to stand
at the boughs of heaven
  gone before me
from out of my womb,
  reborn
    into another confinement
    wider than the whole of my world.